STREET NAMES OF
MILTON KEYNES
CENTRAL

STREET NAMES OF MILTON KEYNES
CENTRAL

ANNE BAKER

Phillimore

2006

Published by
PHILLIMORE & CO. LTD
Shopwyke Manor Barn, Chichester, West Sussex, England
phillimore.co.uk

ISBN 1-86077-409-1
ISBN 13 978-1-86077-409-6

Printed and bound in Great Britain by
THE CROMWELL PRESS
Trowbridge, Wiltshire

CONTENTS

ACKNOWLEDGEMENTS

I would like to thank John Platt, former Secretary to the Board of Milton Keynes Development Corporation, for agreeing to write the Foreword to this book and, as the man originally charged with the task of naming the streets of the new city, making the project possible in the first place. Also, Liz Preston, Milton Keynes City Discovery Centre; Zena Flinn, the Living Archive, Wolverton; and Ruth Meardon, Local Studies Centre, Milton Keynes Library. All those who provided photographs, including David Watts and staff of the Centre for Buckinghamshire Studies; Brett Thorn, Buckinghamshire Museum, and Scott Grace. Not forgetting my family for their support and encouragement and, last but not least, my husband John who wrote the Oldbrook section and the Introduction to this book and helped in so many ways before he died in November 2004.

Dedication

In memory of my husband
John Anthony Baker
1935-2004

FOREWORD

There is a wealth of history in the names in Milton Keynes. They act as a daily reminder of the people who lived in the area through the ages, their way of life, their use of the land and the skills and trades they practised. Sir Frank Markham, in his introduction to the first volume of his *History of Milton Keynes and District* (1973), hoped that the new generation in Milton Keynes might 'wish to know of its past, and to retain the best of it'. Sir Frank was a great believer in the continuity of communities and the value of roots. He had been an opponent of the proposal to build a new town in North Buckinghamshire, but, faced with the decision to go ahead, he and a number of other local people sought to engage with the planners in order to have new development complement the existing settlements. They were particularly anxious to see Stony Stratford and the villages incorporated into the new city in a form they would find acceptable and to make the new city something of which they, too, could be proud. Happily for all concerned, as Michael Reed, later one of the founding Directors of the City Discovery Centre, noted in *The Buckinghamshire Landscape* (1979), the Development Corporation took 'an enlightened attitude towards conservation'.

I remember back in 1973 Sir Frank and Lady Markham walking with Fred Roche, Stuart Mosscrop and Chris Woodward, round the area of the Secklow Mound and down the quiet green lane that ran from Bradwell Common to the Great Linford-Little Woolstone road. Sir Frank, who wanted to impress on the Corporation the long history of the area and the role of the Secklow Hundred as a 'centre of government', was greatly encouraged by the willingness of the designers to listen to his enthusiastic presentation of the past. One of those on this walk was a devotee of the theory of ley lines and would later propose the 'midsummer solstice' pattern of naming for the boulevards. Sir Frank wrote to me in October 1974, a year before he died, expressing the hope 'that my work may in some way help to produce a fine civic consciousness in the great new city'. He never saw the city centre, but I am sure he would have been delighted with the naming of the boulevards and with the incorporation of the Secklow Mound behind the Library.

The names found in Milton Keynes are by no means all from the growth of the new city. Areas like Bradwell, Fenny Stratford, Loughton and Stony Stratford, to name but a few, all contain road names from long before the designation of a new city. So, it was only sensible that, from the beginning, the Development Corporation should have taken naming seriously and welcomed, in 1968, an approach from Newport Pagnell RDC on the question of preserving the history of the area when identifying elements of the new city. Bob Dunbabin, the Clerk of Newport Pagnell RDC, and Ray Bellchambers, then a member of the RDC and a Corporation Board Member, were particularly keen to see the old merged into the new. The Corporation indicated its willingness to take the initiative on naming and I (with a more than passing interest in history) was deputed to do the work. The Local Authorities Joint Liaison Committee endorsed the proposal that the Corporation should take the lead and one of our first acts was to send Sue Godber to see Mr Shirley at Peartree Farm, Woughton-on-the Green, to collect field names; Eaglestone was one of the fruits of this visit.

A small group of MKDC Board Members (Ray Bellchambers, Margaret Durbridge and Jim Cassidy), with a highways engineer (John Rowlands) and myself, devised and put forward the proposals for naming the city areas and the city's H and V roads, and the Board of the Development Corporation cleared the proposals before they were submitted to the local authorities, which had the legal responsibility for such matters. Nearly all the proposals made by the Corporation were accepted, although Wolverton UDC was not happy with the name Hodge Furze and requested a change to Hodge Lea. Those of us who liked the idea of naming the city centre Secklow were over-ruled before any proposals left the Corporation. The local authorities, particularly Newport Pagnell RDC and UDC and Wolverton UDC, played a very helpful part in the process, being keen to conserve all sensible links between the past and the new city's future. Bletchley UDC, which, in my view, was never very enthusiastic about the Development Corporation's role, was unwilling to see defined and named areas created within the UDC boundaries or to anticipate the naming and navigational needs of the wider city road system.

Naming the 'city roads' and CMK 'gates' was one opportunity to conserve long gone aspects of local history, such as Secklow (914), Snelshall Priory (12th century), the Portway (a 13th-century route to Newport), and Groveway (1781). I remember taking the name for Dansteed Way from Dansteed Furlong (Dunstead 1641), mentioned in the book *The Roman Roads of South-East England*. The archaeologists had not yet discovered an ancient settlement in the area – but there was indeed a 'place on the hill', as Dennis Mynard was later happy to tell me! If Dr Margaret Gelling had published her book *Place-Names in the Landscape* (1984) twenty years earlier, we would have been better equipped to spot more significant names from the past.

To 'name' an urban area the size of Milton Keynes was not an easy task. As the opening of new areas and the building of houses gathered pace, the co-operation of developers had to be sought. Some of them were wont to use unimaginative 'catalogue lists' of names for their schemes, which they repeated in towns all over the country. We were ably supported by the new Milton Keynes Borough Council in our efforts to broaden the developers' horizons, the Council sharing our desire to see varied and interesting names adopted. We sought to introduce 'different' themes, particularly in the early years. The Corporation broke new ground with the landscaping of Milton Keynes; we tried in our small way to bring some variety into the naming too.

Pleasing everybody is, of course, impossible, names being a matter of personal taste. It has to be borne in mind that even names low down in the order of things – such as a small residential close on the edge of Milton Keynes – have to be unique if confusion is to be avoided in postal and traffic terms. Producing around 2,000 of them between 1970 and 1992 was not easy; they all had to be cleared by the appropriate councillor as well as by the Council itself. Where did the new city's names come from? Well, many backgrounds, as Anne Baker has recorded so carefully. In the villages history was the usual basis and the Heritage Map (1983), compiled by Bob Croft and Brian Giggins, shows the background to some of the historical names used in the city. Elsewhere themes were selected from which suitable names could emerge, as at Heelands where it was decided to use names from the North-West Yorkshire Highlands, an area with which one of those responsible had a personal family link. Myrtle Bank (Stacey Bushes) reminded me of a hotel in Kingston, Jamaica. Other names were reminiscent of far-flung places known to those involved (in one case a distant holiday home). The 'rock stars' theme at Crownhill was suggested by a local resident who was a member of the Elvis Presley Fan Club, Elvis being 'the King'. Ray Bellchambers made a number of suggestions for names in the Stantonbury and Bradwell areas. The names in Campbell Park were selected in appreciation of the role of Lord Campbell of Eskan in the development of Milton Keynes. Many people made contributions to the bank of names.

Sometimes there were objections. One university-educated resident complained to Wolverton UDC that the name 'Blackdown' at Fullers Slade had unfortunate racial connotations and was unacceptable; he was apparently unaware that the theme was hills and that the Blackdown Hills are in Devon. On another occasion I was asked why such a boringly ordinary name as 'William Smith Close' was used at Woolstone; explanation of the importance of William Smith and his steam plough put that right. Milton Keynes Parish Council invited me to a meeting to explain why such unknown and irrelevant names had been put forward for their village; again, explanation of the historical context of the names was accepted by the villagers. A sign of the times was a reluctance in the early 1970s to see one name attached to a road with both rental and sale housing schemes on it – or even to see the schemes sharing the same access road! By the 1980s such views had disappeared. At Kiln Farm, where the names were in place before many occupants arrived, I received a strong reaction to the spine road being called 'Pitfield'; in this case, the names had been officially approved, but I was told in very straight terms how detrimental to marketing a name like 'Pitfield' would be. I still cannot see the problem (it was after all an old brickmaking area, hence Brickkiln Farm). No London banks seemed to find an address in 'Cheapside' a disadvantage.

One of the last naming tasks I undertook personally, together with highways engineer John Wardley, was the naming of the city road roundabouts. If anyone I meet – in places far from Milton Keynes – has been to the new city, it is the roundabouts they talk about. Despite the Corporation's Information Unit producing city road maps from 1975 and placing Information Boards (incorporating maps) in lay-bys at the entrances to the Designated Area from 1976, the H and V roads and the roundabouts have always defeated some sections of society. We discovered early in the development that lorry drivers mastered map-reading and the navigation system fairly quickly, but those with high-powered cars or higher education found them difficult!

It is hard to believe that it is nearly forty years since the new city project began and it is heartening to see a book incorporating the results of what was essentially a 'backroom' task among the complex and highly technical responsibilities of the Development Corporation. It would be remiss of me not to take the opportunity to acknowledge the contributions made by Ralph Bailey (BMK) and Teresa Jenkins and Val Sharpe (MKDC) over a long period. In addition to their real jobs, they coped with the naming of roads in a multitude of housing developments throughout the new city – a sometimes thankless task, although fascinating to look back on. I also remember well the kindness and support received in the early days from the late Colin Rees, when he was Wolverton UDC's Chief Engineer, and the co-operation received over many years from Dennis Mynard and the staff of the Archaeology Unit.

JOHN PLATT

Secretary to the Board of the
Milton Keynes Development Corporation 1983-92

INTRODUCTION
by John Baker

When in 1967 nearly forty square miles of North Buckinghamshire countryside was designated for the building of Britain's biggest New Town, it was a decision which stirred the emotions of people then living in the three towns and 13 villages in the area.

Many people, particularly those in the northern towns of Wolverton and Stony Stratford, were totally opposed to the concept. Ten miles south, however, the majority of Bletchley residents were far more welcoming, living as they did under an urban authority which had been involved in building 'overspill' accommodation, mainly for Londoners, since shortly after the end of the Second World War.

In 1962, Buckinghamshire's chief architect and planning officer, Fred Pooley, had produced proposals for a city in which the transport system would be based on a monorail with townships of up to 7,000 people built along the route and with no homes more than seven minutes' walk from a station. The object of Pooley's vision was instantly tagged 'Pooleyville' by the local press.

It has been said that Pooley's vision 'laid the foundations' for a future city, although initially it produced considerable squabbling among national, county and local politicians during the early years of the 1960s. This makes it all the more surprising to recall that, by early 1966, the concept finally came into focus in the shape of a map produced by Richard Crossman, Labour's Minister of Housing and Local Government at that time. It revealed an area (later reduced after a public inquiry to 21,900 acres, roughly 34 square miles) on which it was planned to build the biggest New Town of them all, with a population of a quarter of a million people.

Suddenly, speed was of the essence.

Within a matter of months, the Draft North Buckinghamshire New Town (Designation Order) was made and announced by Anthony Greenwood, who had succeeded Crossman. The name Milton Keynes was chosen from one of the villages in the area – a choice strongly supported by Lord Campbell of Eskan, the first appointed Chairman of Milton Keynes Development Corporation, as acknowledging the hybrid of the poet Milton and the internationally acclaimed economist, John Maynard Keynes.

With the appointment of the Main Consultants, Llewelyn-Davies Weeks Forestier-Walker and Bor, and members of the Board of the Corporation, concentration was focused on establishing the key issues affecting the widest range of planning and social objectives, the goals of architects and engineers, the search for vital decisions over the vexed question of the city's transport system, projected housing densities and the siting and size of the new main shopping centre.

Problems on a scale never before encountered were overcome, one by one, as a direct result of the involvement of many of the country's finest planners, architects and engineers gathered together by a Corporation determined to meet the challenges and opportunities presented to make the venture the success it has undoubtedly become.

The Plan for Milton Keynes, which followed an Interim Report a year earlier, was produced for limited distribution among Board members and senior officers late in 1969. Its two volumes were formally launched at a press conference the following March and a Public Inquiry, lasting ten days, took place towards the end of June.

Opposition to the Plan had by now largely dissipated as work began on putting in the first phases of the city's infrastructure. The grid road system as we know it today, started with a section of the H2 (Millers Way) east of the V7 (Saxon Street), there were presentations of plans for specific areas, the first MKDC housing schemes got underway at Simpson and in Stony Stratford, the Open University arrived at Walton Hall, and proposals for the central area of Bletchley and for the two northern towns were presented.

It was all systems go. Then came the shock announcement that the little village of Cublington, near Wing, had been listed among the possible sites for the third London airport. The impact of this news sent shockwaves through most people living in North Buckinghamshire. A poll conducted by the *Milton Keynes Gazette* revealed that more than 90 per cent opposed the plan, which would also have the effect of turning Milton Keynes into an airport city.

The Hon. Mr Justice Roskill, chairing the Commission of Inquiry into the siting of the airport, published plans which would lead to the expansion of Milton Keynes westwards from Bletchley, through Winslow, to provide for a population of more than 400,000 people.

Lord Campbell, who was to earn the soubriquet of 'the father of Milton Keynes', led the fight, strongly supported by press and public, against the proposal which became, for him, a resignation issue. In evidence to the Commission, he went as far as to suggest that grafting an airport onto that part of Milton Keynes which would have been developed by 1987, 'could only produce a mongrel city'. He was subsequently joined in opposition by Professor Colin Buchanan, an architect and town planner who was also a Commission member. His dissenting report ultimately saved the city as we know it today.

Cublington was dropped by the government from the list of possible sites in April 1971 and over the past two decades the plan has become reality.

Development on this scale could only have come about as a result of the participants' belief in the Plan and their collective and individual belief in their abilities, led by a man who was a passionate believer in Milton Keynes.

THE GRID ROADS

The main thoroughfares through Milton Keynes are designed in the pattern of a grid, each square enclosing an estate. The grid roads are numbered vertically – V 1-11 called Streets, and horizontally – H 1-10 called Ways. Even before Roman times, there were several ancient trackways crossing the area which is now Milton Keynes, particularly from west to east, and most of the H Ways have taken their names.

Snelshall Street (V 1)   Refers to Snelshall Priory which stood about a mile and a half to the south-west of nearby Whaddon church. The priory was founded in about 1219 and stood in 11 acres of surrounding countryside.

Tattenhoe Street (V 2)   Named after the tiny village of Tattenhoe, now incorporated in the Tattenhoe area of Milton Keynes. The site of the Norman homestead of Tattenhoe has been preserved.

Fulmer Street (V 3)   Meaning 'the foul mere', Fulmer takes its name from an ancient pond at Shenley Brook End. Also, Fulmoor Close is marked on a 1771 Plan and Survey of Shenley as a field owned by William Brice.

Watling Street (V 4)   This is the section of the old Roman road between Fenny Stratford and Stony Stratford. Until the arrival of Milton Keynes, it was a stretch of the A5 until a new section of the A5 was constructed in the 1970s so that through traffic could have an uninterrupted passage through the new city. The name Watling Street derives from the ninth-century *Waeclinga straet,* meaning 'a Roman road identified with the followers of a man called Wacol', believed to have been centred around St Albans, an early name for which was *Waeclingaceaster.*

Great Monks Street (V 5)   Passes by Bradwell Abbey following the route of an old track along which the monks once traversed.

Grafton Street (V 6)   In the 18th century the Dukes of Grafton (family name Fitzroy) held substantial lands and property in south Northamptonshire, owning several local villages including Deanshanger and Paulerspury. They had a great mansion, Wakefield Lodge, near Potterspury, about a mile from Stony Stratford, where, according to Frank Markham in his *History of Milton Keynes and District,* the Graftons did most of their shopping and tipped the tradesmen with braces of pheasant or partridge. Descended from Charles II, the 3rd Duke was Prime Minister 1768-9 and the 4th Duke (1821-1918) was a well-known local figure.

Saxon Street (V 7)   This street leads to and passes through the centre of Milton Keynes, which is built at the highest point in the area and on the site of Secklow Corner, the ancient Saxon meeting place of the Secklow Hundred.

Marlborough Street (V 8)   The Dukes of Marlborough were associated with the Milton Keynes area after Sarah, Duchess of Marlborough purchased the Stantonbury estates in 1727. She gave it to her grandson, John Spencer, and the lands remained in the ownership of the Earls Spencer of Althorp, Northamptonshire until well into the 19th century. Marlborough Street begins at Stantonbury and skirts the east side of the modern estate.

Overstreet (V 9)   Following the line of a 17th-century track near Downs Barn, this is a short stretch of carriageway connecting Campbell Park with Great Linford. The affix *Over* usually indicates a place 'at the ridge or slope'.

Brickhill Street (V 10)   Named after the villages of Little, Great and Bow Brickhill from where this street begins on its journey northwards to meet the Wolverton road at Great Linford. It replaces an ancient road which ran beside the river Ouzel to Danesborough, an historic hill fort in the woods above Bow Brickhill. According to the *Oxford Dictionary of English Place Names*, Brickhill has nothing to do with bricks, but derives from the Celtic *brig* meaning 'hill top' and the Old English *hyll*.

Tongwell Street (V 11)   Named after the field on which stood Tongwell Farm, shown on an 1806 map of Newport Pagnell. Tongwell Street runs from Old Farm Park to the outskirts of Newport Pagnell.

Ridgeway (H 1)   This is a short section of the prehistoric Ridgeway track which ran from Avebury on Salisbury Plain to the east coast at the Wash.

Millers Way (H 2)   This was the first of the new city roads to be built. It follows the line of an old track which ran between Bradwell windmill and Stony Stratford, hence the name Millers Way.

Monks Way (H 3)   Skirting the site of Bradwell Abbey, this name refers to the monks which once inhabited the abbey and traversed the tracks and pathways in the area.

Dansteed Way (H 4)   Danstead was an ancient site and field name, 'Long Danstead and Short Danstead', shown on a 1678 plan of the area. It is tempting to suggest that the site may have been a homestead occupied by the Danes, but excavations carried out in 1979-81 revealed it to be the site of an Iron-Age/Saxon village. There were, however, many savage raids by the Danes in the early 1000s AD, including an invasion of Newport Pagnell, and several Danish settlements in the area now covered by Milton Keynes. The road runs from Grange Farm in the west to Newport Pagnell.

Portway (H 5)   A Roman route running from Whaddon, through Shenley and Seckloe, to Willen was known by AD 1250 as 'Rector's Portway', and 'Dichefurlong by Portwei'. The new thoroughfare which has taken its name follows close to the old track. Port, meaning a town, or market town, identifies this as 'the way to town' i.e. Newport Pagnell.

Childs Way (H 6) This takes its name from an 18th-century track and field name in east Loughton, by which the road passes on its way from Shenley Common Farm in the east to the M1 at junction 14. An archaic meaning of child (or childe) was a young nobleman. Alternatively, someone named Child(s) may have owned or farmed land in Loughton.

Chaffron Way (H 7) This was the name of an 18th-century track through Woughton, by which the modern Chaffron Way passes. A chaffron, or chamfron, is a piece of leather or plate of steel worn by a horse to protect its face in battle. The reason for its use here is obscure.

Standing Way (H 8) This follows the route of an ancient track which, it is believed, linked Buckingham, via Thornborough, to Watling Street and the Roman station of Magiovinium near Fenny Stratford. Today it is the A421, which runs from Buckingham to the A1, east of Bedford. The name Standing may be a derivation of the Old English word *staning* meaning 'stony places'.

Groveway (H 9) Groveway has been in existence and called by this name since at least the 18th century. It travels from Watling Street at Bletchley to the north side of Wavendon, where it gives way to the ancient London road, coming in from Hockliffe, through Woburn and on to Newport Pagnell. Presumably it once passed through the groves of walnut and other trees which grew in this area.

Bletcham Way (H 10) This was the name of another 18th-century track which passed through Woughton. The name derives from *Blecca's-ham*, the Old English meaning 'homestead of a man called Blecca'. The present road runs from Bletchley to Wavendon Gate.

A Note on OS Map References

The Ordnance Survey (OS) numbers referred to are taken from the Milton Keynes Development Corporation's paper *Names in Milton Keynes* (1992) and are from a 1:2500 scale edition updated in 1965. A collection of old maps may be seen, by appointment, at Milton Keynes City Discovery Centre, Bradwell Abbey, or at the Local Studies Centre, Central Milton Keynes Library.

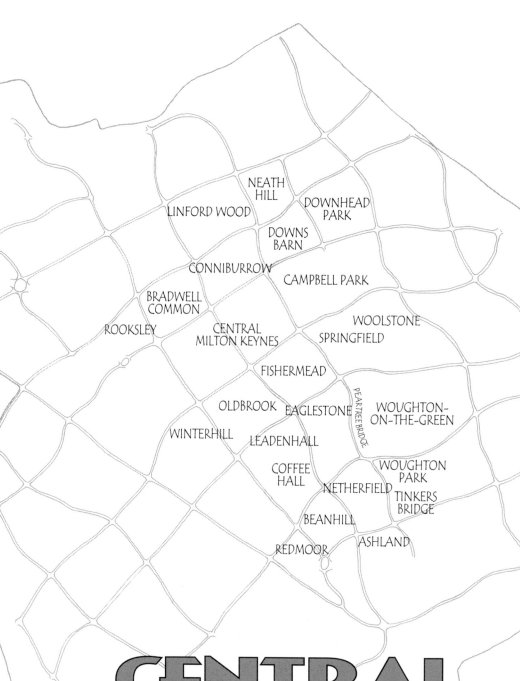

NEATH HILL

DOWNHEAD PARK

LINFORD WOOD

DOWNS BARN

CONNIBURROW

CAMPBELL PARK

BRADWELL COMMON

ROOKSLEY

CENTRAL MILTON KEYNES

WOOLSTONE

SPRINGFIELD

FISHERMEAD

OLDBROOK

EAGLESTONE

WOUGHTON-ON-THE-GREEN

PEARTREE BRIDGE

WINTERHILL

LEADENHALL

COFFEE HALL

WOUGHTON PARK

NETHERFIELD

TINKERS BRIDGE

BEANHILL

REDMOOR

ASHLAND

CENTRAL

ASHLAND

Ashland is an area of parkland with a wet/dry balancing lake. It takes the old name of a field shown on a 1781 map of Simpson, Ordnance Survey maps 41, 46 and 92. For many years Ashland has been the site of the Groveway Greyhound Stadium but this closed down in early 2006 and is awaiting relocation to Elfield Park where a new stadium and facilities is in the process of being built. Ashland is to be a new residential development with planning permission for 360 houses.

BEANHILL

The name 'Beanhill Close' already existed as an old field name on a 1781 map of Simpson, Ordnance Survey map number 20. It denotes that beans were grown here.

THEME **Grasses, food and drink**

Beanfare   Beanfare is the food made from beans, which were a staple part of the Old English diet and widely grown. The beanfeast was an annual dinner which employers gave for their labourers when the fare was mostly beans.

Bungalow housing in Beanfare, Beanhill.

Bracken House   Bracken is a fern, very common in Britain, growing on commons, woodlands and hillsides.

Capron   This is said to be a type of 14th-century strawberry. However, the name seems to suggest a product made from goats' milk. The terms *capric* or *caproic* are applied to fatty acids obtained from butter or cheese with a goat-like smell.

Chervil   Chervil is a herb used in cookery.

Darnel Close   Darnel is a species of rye grass, thought to be the tares mentioned in the Bible. It is supposed to contain narcotic properties.

Dodkin   A dodkin was a form of pot-cake made from barley.

Lammas   Lammas Day on 1 August is a cross-quarter-day in England and a regular quarter-day in Scotland. In Anglo-Saxon days it was the time when the first fruits of labour were offered. It was a sort of harvest festival and bread for the Lammas Day eucharist was made from the newly cut corn. The name Lammas comes from the Old English *hlaf-maesse*, meaning 'the loaf-mass'.

Marram Close   Marram is a seaside grass, often seen growing out of sand dunes.

Maslin Drive   Maslin is a mix of rye and wheat grain, the flour of which was used to make maslin bread.

Medale Road   Mead-ale was an ale made with mead, which was honey and water that had been fermented and flavoured.

Melick Road   Melic is a grass of the fescue family which includes many pasture and fodder grasses.

Neapland   Neepland (variant spelling) was a field where turnips or 'neeps' were grown.

Simnel   A simnel cake was a rich, sweet cake traditionally eaten on Mothering Sunday (mid-Lent) in remembrance of the feeding of the five thousand and of the feast held by Joseph for his brethren. The simnel cake was decorated with scallops. Simila was the finest wheat flour, and simnel bread was also made.

Tandra   Tandra cakes, or Tandrew Whigs, were small cakes once eaten on St Andrew's Day, particularly in Buckinghamshire and Bedfordshire.

Wastel   Wastel was a bread made from very fine flour.

Wheatcroft Close   This was the name of a field in this area. Wheat is a type of corn, most commonly used to make bread and cake flour. A croft is a small piece of arable land attached to a dwelling, or a small farm.

Woodrush Close   The woodrush is a type of rush which grows in woodlands. It is of the genus Luzula, the same family as true rushes.

BRADWELL COMMON

Bradwell Common is the traditional name of this area.

Arbrook Avenue   Arbrook Common is one of the Elmbridge commons in the Esher area of Surrey. It is ancient common land of ornithological interest lying south of Esher within the triangle of Esher Common, Oxshott Heath and Epsom.

Blackheath Crescent   Blackheath Common in south London is on the borders of Greenwich Park, which is part of Greenwich World Heritage Site. Once ancient common land used for grazing, in 1944 the Blackheath Society protested against gravel pits on the common being filled with bomb-site rubble. More recently, the common was saved from destruction by local protests against plans to run a motorway through it. Fringed by Blackheath Village with its many pubs and restaurants, the common today is a wide expanse of grassland, popular with kite flyers.

Booker Avenue   Booker Common is off the M40 at the south-western corner of High Wycombe, Buckinghamshire. Booker Gliding Centre is situated there.

Bradwell Common Boulevard   This is the central road through the estate.

Brill Place   Brill Common in Buckinghamshire has a long and ancient history. In the 13th century, craftsmen potters had a production centre at Brill and they became market leaders in their industry. They obtained their clay from Brill Common and their diggings changed the shape of the landscape, pitting it with the grassy hollows seen there today. Remains of their 13th- and 14th-century brick kilns have been discovered. The windmill on the common was built in 1680 and rebuilt in 1948. Standing 600 feet above sea level, open to all weathers in this cold and windy place, it was used for milling barley until 1919.

Burnham Drive   Burnham in Buckinghamshire is best known for Burnham Beeches, north of the village, which are the remains of a primeval forest which once covered much of Buckinghamshire. The average age of the pollarded beech trees is over 400 years, and the largest tree, known as the Druids' Oak, is believed to be over 800 years old and its girth, measured half a metre above ground level, is over 30 feet.

Chesham Avenue   Chesham Bois Common in Buckinghamshire covers about forty acres of amenity woodlands with bridle and footpaths, dells and two large open spaces, one of which has a pond, the other a cricket pitch which has been used for over 100 years by the Chesham Bois village cricket club. Since 1992 a large part of the common has been included in the Chesham

Bois conservation area, defined as an area of special architectural or historical interest. At the beginning of the 20th century, the common was an open space with a few trees, bracken and gorse and a number of small ponds and dells. In 1919 the landscape was changed when new trees were planted and over the years self-seeded ash and sycamore created more woodland. Many of the trees now are oak, hornbeam, wild cherry, holly and hawthorn.

Clapham Place   Clapham Common in south-west London covers 220 acres of wide open space. It has a small lake, a couple of ponds, a bandstand and play areas and sports facilities.

Coleshill Place   Coleshill Common lies south-west of Amersham in Buckinghamshire. The village of Coleshill once had lace and red earthenware industries and a windmill on the common.

Dorney Place   Dorney Common near Windsor covers 200 acres. With bridle paths and a stream running through, it marks the county boundary between Berkshire and Buckinghamshire.

Eelbrook Avenue   Eelbrook Common is in Fulham, London. The 13 acres of park and tennis courts was for centuries a piece of swampy wasteland, variously called mutations of 'Hillebrooke'. In 1727 it was described as of little use or benefit and in need of a clean-up and proper maintenance. By the 19th century improvements had been made and its present name became appropriate. It was said that a large ditch around the area and another across it were well stocked with carp, tench, roach and eels.

Forrabury Avenue   The only Forrabury found is at Boscastle in Cornwall, which seems a little far away from here. Forrabury Common is high above the village and is, remarkably, still farmed by the old Celtic strip system known locally as 'stickmeal' cultivation, from the word *stich* meaning in rows or lines.

Hadley Place   Hadley Common, or Monken Hadley Common, is just north of London, near Barnet. Ancient common and woodland in a green belt area, it is now under threat from proposals to build a new railway station and car park close by. Comedian Spike Milligan lived there.

Hampstead Gate   Hampstead Heath, known as 'the lungs of London', is one of the best known of all north London commons. From Parliament Hill, one of the highest points of the common, there are views right across London. The several small lakes and ponds were formed from the pits left after the extraction of clay for brick making in the 19th century. Now they are used for bathing, fishing and boating. Kenwood House on the northern fringe was built in the early 18th century and remodelled and enlarged by Robert Adam. It was the home of Lord Mansfield, the Lord Chief Justice, and now stands in an acre owned by English Heritage. A Bronze-Age barrow has been landscaped with trees to make a special feature.

Ibstone Avenue   High on the Chiltern Hills in Buckinghamshire is Ibstone village and common. A long street runs down one side of the common with flint and brick cottages against a backdrop of beech woods. A windmill in the village was used in the film *Chitty Chitty Bang Bang*.

Leasowe Place   Leasowe Common in the Wirral, Cheshire has a lighthouse which is a well-known landmark. Standing 101 feet high, the lighthouse has seven floors, a cast-iron staircase of 137 steps climbing to each. A base for coastal rangers, it ceased to function in the early 20th century.

Maidenhead Avenue   Maidenhead is a fine old Berkshire town on the Thames with a graceful bridge by Brunel carrying the railway across the river, but the common seems to be a place of the past, except for remnants of common land in outskirt villages such as Pinkneys Green. Wildbrook Common between Maidenhead and Cookham is a large, wild area with a brook running through it.

Mayditch Place   No information available.

Mitcham Place   Mitcham Common in south London covers 460 acres of the borough of Merton. Important for nature conservation, it includes secondary woodland, grassland, scrub and ponds. There was once a post mill, built in 1806, which was working until 1860. It was struck by lightning in about 1875 when two sails were destroyed, and the mill was demolished in 1915 leaving a few ruins which can still be seen.

Naphill Place   Naphill near High Wycombe, Buckinghamshire is a registered common. Consisting of woodland and heathland, it is an ancient tree site of oak and beech pollards.

Plumstead Avenue   Plumstead Common is in south-east London. In 1991 the Plumstead Common Environment Group was formed by a small group of people who were concerned about the lack of care of the common and its woodland, which had become an unofficial rubbish dump. They now work with Greenwich Council to conserve and maintain the area. It took two years to clear and restore the severely polluted Slade Ponds, to which wildfowl have now returned, and the work earned the group a Shell Best of Better Britain Award. Sadly, though, the common still suffers from vandalism and the dumping of burnt-out cars.

Stokenchurch Place   Stokenchurch Common, on the Buckinghamshire/ Oxfordshire border, is a wide open space crossed by many footpaths, including the Ridgeway path. Red kites may be seen here and the area was chosen by Bill Oddie as the site for his television documentary on the bird. At 750 feet above sea level, there was once a post mill here which was demolished in the early 20th century.

Streatham Place   Streatham Common in south-west London is a large green space with wooded areas and tennis courts. The Friends of Streatham Common Group organise events such as children's shows, fetes, performances of Shakespeare's plays and an annual Kite Day. Public gardens nearby known as The Rookery were once part of the grounds of a large house which was demolished during the early 1900s. The White Garden, which has white benches and only white flowers, was a favourite spot of Queen Mary.

Tylers Green   There is a common around the village of Tylers Green near Penn in Buckinghamshire. The area was known as a centre for the production of tiles, particularly medieval glazed floor tiles. Archaeologists recently unearthed a substantial post-medieval tile kiln, a structure with tiled walls and a number of glazed floor tiles and pottery at a site near Rose Cottage, Tylers Green.

Walkhampton Avenue   Walkhampton Common is on the south-western edge of Dartmoor, on the river Walkham near Yelverton. An expansive wilderness strewn with rocks and sheep, which are hard to tell apart, an occasional stumpy tree or weather-beaten bush and an undulating horizon topped with rocky tors, the area resembles the surface of the moon or Mars.

Wandsworth Place   In south-west London, Wandsworth Common covers 175 acres with ecological and ornamental features. An urban green space with grassland, woodland and pond habitats, part of the common is managed for wildlife and the rest as a community amenity. There is a lake with fishing in season, sports pitches, tennis, bowling, and a children's playground.

Wimbledon Place   Wimbledon Common of Womble fame is in the London borough of Wandsworth. Wimbledon Windmill, restored in 1976, and Museum are on an area of the common which is managed as a Site of Special Scientific Interest to conserve a wide variety of birds, insects, animals and plants. There are nature trails, golf courses, bridleways and cycle paths. Adjacent to Richmond Park and Putney Common, together the whole area covers about 1,140 acres of countryside, with heathland, woodland and scrubland.

Wisley Avenue   Wisley Common in Surrey cannot be said to be 'off the beaten track'. At the intersection of the M25 and A3, it is only a few metres away from busy roads. Nevertheless, nature thrives on this large area of wet heathland, with birch and pine woodland, many dragonflies, interesting bog plants and fruiting cotton grass in midsummer.

CAMPBELL PARK

Built on the eastern slope of Bradwell Common, Campbell Park is named in memory of 'the father of Milton Keynes', The Rt Hon The Lord Campbell of Eskan, who was appointed first Chairman of the Milton Keynes Development Corporation in 1967. Born on 8 August

1912, 'Jock' Campbell, as he was affectionately known, was educated at Eton and Exeter College, Oxford before working for a short time at the Colonial Office. In 1934 he joined the family firm, Curtis Campbell & Co., working on the sugar plantation in British Guiana (now Guyana). In 1939 the firm, and Jock Campbell with it, was bought by Booker McConnell Ltd. Rising through the ranks to Chairman in 1952, he was knighted in 1957, created Lord Campbell of Eskan on 14 January 1966 and retired from Bookers in 1967, though he retained many connections with the West Indies, such as his Presidency of the West India Committee and Chairmanship of the Commonwealth Sugar Exporters Group. His special concerns were the economic and social problems of developing countries, and race relations. His hobbies included reading, painting and golf, and he was an expert at crossword puzzles. Lord Campbell died on Boxing Day, 26 December 1994.

THEME **Lord Campbell's Association with the Sugar Industry in Guyana**
(Bookers' interests in Guyana were acquired by the Guyanese Government in 1976)

Adelphi Street   Adelphi, from the Greek word *Adelphoi,* meaning brothers, is the name of a small, fashionable area of central London developed by the Adams brothers in the 18th century. The Adelphi sugar plantation in Berbice, Guyana was once owned by Quintin Hogg and his partners. The Campbell and Hogg families were business partners in Demerara in the 19th century.

Albion Place   The Albion sugar estate in Berbice, Guyana was owned by the Campbell family in the early 20th century, and later acquired by Bookers. It was first cultivated in the late 18th century for the growing of cotton, but was later developed as a model sugar estate and factory. Some of the large turbines were supplied by

The Rt Hon. the Lord Campbell of Eskan, Chairman of the Milton Keynes Development Corporation.

Allens of Bedford. Albion, or Albany, is an ancient name for Great Britain, commonly believed to have originated from the white cliffs of the coast of Kent, where Jock Campbell spent some of his young life. Also, there is an area in the central Highlands of Scotland called Breadalbane, meaning 'the upper part of Albany or Albion', which was once owned by the Campbell clan.

Avebury Boulevard   See Central Milton Keynes.

Blairmont Street   Blairmont is a town close to the east coast of Guyana. The Blairmont sugar estate in Berbice was founded in the 18th century by a man named Blair. It was owned by the Davson family for more than 100 years, before it became a Booker estate in 1939.

Canal Side   On the eastern fringe of Campbell Park, beside the Grand Union canal.

Colgrain Street   Colgrain, near Helensburgh in Dumbartonshire, was the home of Lord Campbell's family in the 19th and early 20th centuries.

Columbia Place   Columbia was a sugar plantation in Essequibo, close to Plantation Reliance.

Dalgin Place   Dalgin was an early plantation on the banks of the river Demerara, some 55 miles south of Georgetown. Today it is just a Guyanese village.

Enmore Gate   Enmore, a sugar estate in Demerara, was owned by Bookers during the 20th century. Growing cotton in the late 18th century, by 1883 it was regarded as 'the most successful pioneer estate in the colony'. During the American Civil War it briefly reverted to cotton.

Enterprise Lane   Enterprise was a sugar plantation in Demerara associated with Bookers.

Eskan Court   The Eskan area of Scotland was Lord Campbell's homeland. Camis-Eskan House is at Colgrain.

Glenstal Place   This refers to Glenstal Abbey (now a school) near Limerick, Ireland. Lord Campbell's maternal grandfather was High Sheriff of County Limerick and, as a four-year-old in 1916, Jock Campbell was sent to stay with his grandparents in Limerick to escape the Zeppelin raids during the First World War.

Highbury Lane   Highbury, an area of London, was the name given to a Booker sugar plantation in Berbice.

Huntley Crescent   Huntley was the name of a sugar plantation in Demerara, associated with Bookers in the early 19th century.

Mara Place   Mara was originally a coffee plantation in Berbice, but later was noted for its sugar and cocoa.

Melville Street   Also owned by Bookers, Melville was a sugar plantation in Demerara. It incorporated an old plantation known as Strath Campbell.

Montrose Street   A historic town on Scotland's east coast, at the entrance to the tidal Montrose Basin, which name was given to a sugar plantation owned by Bookers in Demerara, the name of a river and district in east Guyana.

The cricket pavilion, Campbell Park.

Overgate This is a gateway road from Overstreet into, and crossing over, the parkland area of Campbell Park.

Pilgrim Street The Plantation de Pilgrim, founded in the 1740s, was one of the first coastal estates in Essequibo, the name of a river and a district in Guyana.

Reliance Lane Reliance was the name given to a sugar plantation owned by the Campbell family in Essequibo.

Silbury Boulevard See Central Milton Keynes.

Skeldon Gate Skeldon is a sugar estate in the Corentyne district of Berbice. It was owned by Bookers in the 20th century, and small turbines were supplied to the estate by Allens of Bedford. The name is of Scottish origin, the Skeldon estate being in Dalrymple, Ayrshire, where there is a fine golf course and club house.

Smithsons Place Smithson's Place was a 'once comfortable and prosperous' sugar plantation in the Canje district of Berbice, for which Bookers were the agents.

Taymouth Place Taymouth Manor was a sugar plantation in Essequibo. Taymouth Castle, on the south bank of the river Tay, was once the seat of the Campbells of Breadalbane. The present early 19th-century castle, built by John Campbell, 1st Marquis of Breadalbane, incorporates part of an older 16th-century castle, which fell into ruin.

CENTRAL MILTON KEYNES

Built on what was wild and windy Bradwell Common, the highest point of the Milton Keynes designated area, Central Milton Keynes contains all the amenities one would expect of a major city centre. At the east end of the massive glass shopping mall with its two-and-a-half miles of shop-lined walkways, the 155 feet high snowdrome of the Xscape leisure and entertainments complex dominates the skyline above the theatre district, while at the west end, the dome of the Church of Christ the Corner Stone rises over the hotels and business area which sweeps down towards the law courts, police station and railway station.

THEME **The area's Saxon origins and later history**

Avebury Boulevard   Avebury village in Wiltshire lies on the site of an extensive complex of Neolithic and early Bronze-Age stone circles, banks and ditches. The ditch and outer bank of the main circle encloses an area of more than 30 acres and two smaller circles lie within it.

Bouverie Square   In the business area of Central Milton Keynes, this is named after Bouverie Street in the City of London, which was named after the wealthy Bouverie family who purchased the land there in the 16th century.

Elder Gate   An elder was a senior member of a Saxon tribe; a highly respected community leader. The modern term 'alderman' is derived from it.

Grafton Gate and Grafton Park   As with Grafton Street, the V6 grid-road, this refers to the Dukes of Grafton, whose residence was a large mansion at Wakefield near Potterspury and who owned most of south Northamptonshire. In the 18th century the Grafton Hunt was founded by

The V8 Marlborough Street grid-road, passing between Central Milton Keynes and Campbell Park.

26

The Church of Christ the Corner Stone, Central Milton Keynes.

the Duke of Grafton. Its country included the Whaddon Chase, Brackley and Towcester and the hunt kennels were at Wakefield Lodge.

Marlborough Gate   Leading off the V8 Marlborough Street grid-road, this was named after the Duke of Marlborough who married Sarah Jennings, one time owner of the lands of Stantonbury.

Midsummer Boulevard   When designing the alignment of the three main boulevards for Central Milton Keynes, the planners noticed that their orientation equated with the line between the midsummer sunrise and midsummer sunset, that of the midsummer solstice.

North Row   A row running west to east along the north side of the city centre.

Saxon Gate   The Saxons were a west Germanic people who invaded, raided and settled parts of south Britain. Their reign spanned the fifth and sixth centuries AD during which time the area now covered by Central Milton Keynes was included in the Saxon hundred of Sigelai, or Seckloe(w) as it was later called. It was the custom in Saxon times for the families of a hundred to meet at the highest point in their area, which in the Seckloe Hundred was Bradwell Common, probably where the shopping centre now stands, although a mound behind the library is popularly believed to have been the spot.

Secklow Gate   Named with deference to the Saxon Secklow Hundred, which covered most of the Milton Keynes designated area. The name, which has mutated over the centuries from Sigelai to Seggelawe in 1280, through Secklo and Segehowe and others, originally meant 'warrior's hill'. It was a prerequisite of the Saxon hundreds that their courts and meetings should be held at an accessible, high, central point at the junction of several tracks or footpaths, and preferably sheltered by a great oak or two. Bradwell Common, being just such a spot, was where the hundred or so families of the Secklow Hundred held their assemblies.

Silbury Boulevard Silbury Hill is a prehistoric mound in Wiltshire. Its construction began in about 2150 BC and, at 130 feet high, it is the largest man-made hill in Europe. The name was chosen because of its association with the summer solstice and Avebury stone circles.

South Row A row running west to east on the south side of the city centre.

South Second and Fourth – Tenth Streets, North Second – Fourteenth Streets, Upper Second, Fourth and Fifth Streets, Lower Second, Fourth and Eighth – Twelfth Streets Mainly office blocks, all these streets follow the American style of street naming, aiding the cosmopolitan ambience the planners wished to create.

Still growing – development in Central Milton Keynes, with the construction of Solstice House, at the junction of Midsummer Boulevard and Witan Gate. Developed by Queens Moat Properties, Solstice House is a 30,000 square foot headquarters building.

Station Square The square in front of the railway station.

Witan Gate A witan was a body of 30-40 high-ranking laymen and ecclesiastics which advised Anglo-Saxon kings on political matters such as foreign policy and taxation. It only met at the king's behest and followed no particular procedure. The witan also acted as a court, hearing cases on matters affecting the king and other important people.

The Shopping Centre

THEME The Armorial Bearings of the Borough of Milton Keynes

Acorn Walk Referring to the acorns of the oak tree, which is the main charge of the shield.

Borough Walk A walkway leading to and from the Civic Offices of the Borough Council, the name alluding to the arms of the Borough of Milton Keynes.

View of the Central Milton Keynes Shopping Centre from the Belvedere, Campbell Park.

City Square   From the beginning, Milton Keynes was referred to as 'the New City', a concept which has been disputed by some who argue that to qualify as a city there must be a cathedral. However, according to the *Chambers Dictionary*, a city can also be defined 'in various countries' as a 'municipality of higher rank' such as 'the business centre or original area of a large town'.

Crown Walk   A mural crown encircles the oak tree on the shield.

Deer Walk   A shield on the arms is supported by two bucks, or male deer. The name also serves to commemorate the herds of deer which once roamed the common land on which the shopping centre is built.

Eagle Walk   The Borough crest contains a Roman eagle. In mythology, the eagle represents the sun, which befits the solstitial orientation of the shopping centre.

East Walk   The walkway, or promenade, through the east side of Midsummer Place.

Field Walk   The field is the basic background of the shield. This is also a reminder that the shopping centre was built on the fields of Bradwell Common.

Gold Oak Walk   There is an oak tree on the shield and oak branches on the crest, both of which are coloured gold.

Helmet Walk   Above the shield is a metal protective head cover, the helm, on which stands the crest.

Market Square   The square where the market is held.

Middleton Hall   The middle name of John (Jock) Middleton Campbell, created Lord Campbell of Eskan on 14 January 1966, who was the original Chairman of Milton Keynes Development Corporation. Officially, however, this spacious hall takes the original Saxon name, Middleton, from which Milton is derived, and means 'the middle of the town'.

Midsummer Arcade   One of the two main shopping malls, this runs parallel to Midsummer Boulevard and, likewise, takes its name from its alignment with the midsummer solstice.

Midsummer Place   So called because of the natural alignment with the midsummer solstice, and its proximity to Midsummer Boulevard, this extension to the shopping centre was opened in October 2000, creating a total shopping area of 1.6 million square feet.

Oak Court   Here stands an ancient oak tree, reputed to be 170 years old, preserved in its unnatural surroundings. At its base are oak leaves and acorns sculpted in bronze by local artist Tim Ward.

A view across Central Milton Keynes from the roof of Exchange House showing the Shopping Building (left) and the Point multiplex entertainment centre (to the right).

Queens Court   Originally The Garden Court, this square was renamed in deference to Queen Elizabeth II, who visited the shopping centre building in 1979. Here the solar connection continues. The court forms a perfect square and into the paving is carved a circle upon which four bollards mark the cardinal points of the compass. Four more bollards on the circle indicate the direction towards sunrise and sunset at the summer and winter solstices, when viewed from the centre of the circle. A sundial near a pool shows the time of day and, by the length of the shadow, indicates the date on a series of arcs engraved on the dial.

Silbury Arcade   One of the two main shopping malls, this runs parallel to Silbury Boulevard and, likewise, takes its name from Silbury Hill in Wiltshire.

South Concourse   At the southern end of Midsummer Place, this concourse is at the confluence of the east and west walkways.

Sunset Walk   At the western end of the shopping centre's Midsummer Arcade, this marks the position of the setting sun.

The Boulevard   In Midsummer Place, the Boulevard is a large and airy broadwalk given over almost entirely to cafés and restaurants. Designed to encapsulate the ambience of a Parisian boulevard with its open-air cafés, it is named in the French style – a boulevard being a wide road, or promenade, usually lined with trees and, sometimes, cafés as well.

West Walk   The walkway, or promenade, through the west side of Midsummer Place.

The Theatre District

Atrium   Here a circle at the centre of the theatre district, the atrium was the main court of a Roman house, or the court in front of an early Christian church. It is also the name of the upper chamber of the heart and, in general, pertains to the centre or heart of something.

Garrick Walk   The Garrick is a London theatre named after David Garrick 1717-79, famous actor, manager and dramatist. He began his acting career in an East End of London theatre, achieving stardom with his portrayal of Richard III and quickly advancing to Drury Lane. He is buried in Westminster Abbey and is still regarded as the most versatile actor in British stage history. The Garrick Club in London was named after him.

Margaret Powell Square   Margaret Powell was a local landowner. She set up a trust fund for the elderly and disabled people of Milton Keynes to enable them to enjoy as many of the city's amenities as possible. The theatre was equipped with money from the fund and has the best facilities for the disabled of any theatre in the UK.

Piazza   A piazza is the Italian version of a plaza, a large open space or square.

Plaza   A plaza is an open space or square, especially in Spain. In the USA it is used to denote a modern complex of shops, cafés and parking areas.

Savoy Crescent   The Savoy Theatre in London was built at the instigation of Richard D'Oyly Carte especially for the staging of Gilbert and Sullivan's operas. It first opened in October 1881 with a performance of *Patience* and was the first public building ever to be illuminated by electric lighting. The auditorium was rebuilt in 1929 and became a listed building, but was destroyed by fire in 1990. It now stands again, the 1929 building having been recreated.

Theatre Walk   A walkway by the theatre.

COFFEE HALL

Coffee Hall is named after Coffee Hall Farm, which stood beside Peartree Lane and is shown on Ordnance Survey map 16.

THEME **The historic Coffee Houses of London**

The first coffee house opened in London in 1652 and they quickly spread, satisfying both a social and a business need in the everyday life of the City for the next 200 years. In 1873-74 petitions were raised against coffee houses, women protesting that they made men 'as unfruitful as the desert', and coffee became known as 'ninny-broth' and 'turkey-gruel'. There were also attempts by governments to suppress the coffee houses, feared as hot-beds of subversive talk and scandalous gossip. They certainly had their seamy side, but many of the business institutions we take for granted today have their origins in the 17th- and 18th-century coffee houses. The Post Office, the Fire Service, insurance schemes, the Bank of England, even the newspaper Box Number began life in the coffee houses.

Button Grove   Button's Coffee House in Russell Street, Covent Garden was opened in about 1712/13 by Daniel Button with the financial aid of Joseph Addison, founder and editor of *The Spectator*. Daniel was previously a servant to the Countess of Warwick, whom Addison married in 1716. Button's became famous for the lion's head letter-box which opened its mouth to receive the items posted in it. It was also renowned as the centre of literature, the clientele being the celebrated writers, poets and wits of the day. These included Sir Richard Steele, writer, politician and founder of *The Tatler*. Button died in 1731, but the coffee house continued until about 1750. The lion's head letter-box was moved to another site before being bought in 1837 by the Duke of Bedford and taken to Woburn Abbey, where it may well still be.

Chapter From the early 18th century, Chapter Coffee House was in
Paternoster Row. It was frequented by booksellers, writers and men
of letters, and the clergy, and was noted for its supply of newspapers,
pamphlets and books. A reading society was formed with some meetings
being attended by James Boswell and Dr Samuel Johnson. By 1781 a
chemical society met there, indicating that scientists and chemists were
among the clientele. But Chapter was best known for its library, for it took
in and stored newspapers from across England and from France as well
as files of important papers. The library was supported by subscription.
Chapter was closed in about 1853.

Copperfield School Charles Dickens was a customer of many of the London
coffee houses in the 1800s and several of them are mentioned by name in
his writings, or used as settings in his novels. In *David Copperfield* he uses
Gray's Inn Coffee House as the place where David lodges on his return from
abroad.

Daniels Welch Daniels Welch was another of Fleet Street's many coffee
houses. The Heralds from the College of Arms were to be found here and,
according to a contemporary account, 'the conversation was mainly of
pedigrees and descents'. In 1722 it was being frequented by the Freemasons
Company and used as a masonic lodge meeting place.

Elfords Elford's Coffee House, George Yard, Lombard Street is reliably
documented as existing in the 1670s. Sales of goods salvaged from
shipwrecks were held here in the 1680s. The proprietor in the 1690s was
John Elford, son of one of the earliest coffeemen. He was a good friend
of Edward Lloyd of Lloyd's Coffee House and shared a similar breed of
customer, centred on commercial shipping interests. Kept at Elford's was
the account of Alexander Selkirk's castaway adventure on Fernando Island,
on which Defoe based his *Robinson Crusoe*. It seems that Elford's was
probably burned down in the Cornhill fire of 1748.

Garraways Garraway's Coffee House was opened in Exchange Alley,
Cornhill in about 1670 by Thomas Garraway. Here the fur traders of
the Hudson Bay Company sold their beaver coats and skins. Over the
roughly 200 years of its history, Garraway's was the scene of a variety of
commercial exchanges. Wines were sold, ships were auctioned, insurance
policies traded, tickets for monthly music concerts, polished diamonds, 'true
Spanish roll'd Tobacco', all were advertised as obtainable. It was also a
place where rewards could be obtained for the return of lost valuables, with
'no questions asked'. As with many of the coffee houses, from 1752 to 1850
it was used as a business address by all sorts of traders, stockbrokers and
bank directors. Auctions were held of sugar, textiles, timber and salvaged
goods, and property auctions and Sales by the Candle, which is to offer
for sale for as long as a small candle burns, took place. By the beginning

of the 19th century, Garraway's was less of a coffee house and more of a trading establishment, with large rooms for the sale of ships, estates and commodities. It disappeared some time during the 19th century.

Grigsby Rise   Grigsby's Coffee House was in Threadneedle Street, near the Royal Exchange. Probably established between 1700-6, it was used as an auction room. A collection of pictures was sold here in 1720. It also sold theatre tickets and fire insurance and was used by merchants, brokers, wax-bleachers and dealers in general merchandise as a trading address up until about 1833, after which it seems to have disappeared.

Hamlins   Hamlins Coffee House was in Sweetings Alley, Cornhill. It is recorded that in 1702-14 the conversation at Hamlins was about infant baptism, lay ordination and other religious matters, indicating that it was frequented by the clergy. In 1759 Hamlins was destroyed by yet another fire in Cornhill, which had started in a room at Hamlins. It seems to have been rebuilt, for between 1767-80 traders such as merchants and distillers were using the premises.

Jonathans   Jonathan's Coffee House in Exchange Alley, Cornhill is believed to have been opened in about 1680 by Jonathan Miles. The premises were used by brokers and dealers in stocks and shares, in preference to the nearby Royal Exchange. Jonathan's was also frequented by Joseph Addison, founder and editor of *The Spectator*. In 1710 he reported, 'I have been taken for a merchant on the Exchange ... and sometimes pass for a Jew in the assembly of Stock-Jobbers at Jonathan's'. It was also a great venue for speculators. A fire in Cornhill in 1748 destroyed the original Jonathan's but it was quickly rebuilt only to perish finally in another fire in 1778.

Lloyds   Lloyd's Coffee House was first opened round about the 1680s by Edward Lloyd in Tower Street, London, but moved in 1691 to Lombard Street. Although he was known as 'Mr Lloyd the Coffeeman', the business conducted from the coffee house involved far more than serving coffee. The shipping fraternity gathered there and ships were bought and sold, money-raising projects were discussed, underwriting was undertaken and shipping intelligence gleaned. In 1693 Mr Lloyd was paid £3 by the Hudson Bay Shipping Company for intelligence on the company's ships. From these beginnings evolved the famous Lloyds Underwriters and international insurance market. By 1773 Lloyd's Coffee House was in decline, relying on selling and serving coffee until its demise in 1785.

Robins Hill   Robin's Coffee House in Exchange Alley, Cornhill was described in 1702 as a 'Stock-Jobbing coffee-house'. Among various money-raising schemes run at Robin's was an insurance office to cover horses in cases of natural death, becoming disabled or being stolen. Daniel Defoe described Robin's in 1722 as 'the resort of foreign bankers, and often, even of foreign ministers'. It is believed to have closed some time in the 1740s.

Rochfords   Rochford's Chocolate and Coffee House by Charing Cross was kept by Mrs (or 'Madame') Rochford in the early 18th century. The Charing Cross area was less commercial than the City and its coffee houses attracted the professional people and the socialites of the day. Rochford's was frequented by the *beau monde* and, possibly, men of the professions.

St Dunstans   St Dunstans Coffee House was in Fleet Street and was probably opened in the second half of the 17th century. On 12 January 1715 a meeting was held there attended by a Mr Henry Hoare, banker and goldsmith, who suggested the foundation of Westminster Hospital. The Fleet Street coffee houses were frequented by bankers, lawyers, doctors and the clergy, which were highly likely to have made up the clientele of St Dunstans. In 1741 the premises were advertised to let with a wine vault beneath it, good cellaring and other conveniences.

Serles Close   Serle's Coffee House in Lincoln's Inn possibly derived its name from Henry Serle, who died in 1690, or from Serle Street, on the corner of which it stood. It was frequented by 'gentlemen of the law', civil servants and politicians. The Bloomsbury and Inns of Court Association held its meetings there and it provided 'good soups, dinners and beds'. Serle's appears to have been cleared away in a rebuilding programme around 1897.

Squires Close   Squires Coffee House in Fulwoods Rents, Holborn was possibly opened by a Mr Squiar around the 1670/80s. He was a noted coffeeman who died in 1717. The early Squires Coffee House was patronised by the law students of Gray's Inn. Books were sold here as well as theatre tickets. Among the clientele was Sir Roger de Coverley, who in 1711 entertained Joseph Addison, founder and editor of *The Spectator*, here.

Trubys Gardens   Truby's Coffee House in St Paul's Churchyard is believed to have been part of the *Queens Arms Tavern*, the proprietors of which in 1712 were the Messrs Trubey. According to Jonathan Swift (author of *Gulliver's Travels*), writing in 1713, town and country vicars flocked in tribes to Truby's, where they exchanged clerical gossip.

Virginia   There were numerous Virginia Coffee Houses in London between 1660 and 1840. Their name derived from the new colony of Virginia, which was being settled during the 18th century. They were mainly frequented by those involved with the colony's trade – merchants, ship owners and ships' captains, and all manner of traders. Also in the 18th century, fire insurance companies held their meetings in the Virginia Coffee Houses in the Cornhill area. At The Virginia in Threadneedle Street in 1728, the sale of a Negro boy aged 11 years was advertised, and in 1734 'the largest rattle snake ever seen in England and just arrived from Virginia' was put on show. A year later it was joined by a foot-long scorpion from Angola.

CONNIBURROW

Named after 'Connie Burrough Hill', shown on a 1641 map of Great Linford. The Old English word 'borough' meant to protect or shelter. A cony was a small, burrowing animal of the hare family. Conniburrow was built on part of what was Bradwell Common, where there were many rabbit, or cony, burrows.

THEME **Wild Flowers**

Bramble Avenue   The bramble is of the rose family and commonly known as the blackberry bush, a scrambling, thorny plant with white, rose-like flowers in summer and blackberry fruits in early autumn. In the Middle Ages the fruit juice was used to make wine and was added to grape wine as a sweetener.

Bryony Place   The White Bryony is of the gourd family. A climbing perennial which grows to four metres, It has greenish-white flowers from May to September and red berries and tendrils, like ringlets, at the nodes. The Black Bryony is of the yam family. Also a climber, it twines clock-wise and has no tendrils. It has dark green shiny leaves, tiny yellow-green flowers and red berries. It grows in hedges, woods and scrubland.

Carlina Place   Carlina is the Latin name for the Carline Thistle, a low-growing, short and spiny thistle with yellow-brown flower heads and yellow bracts which resemble sun rays and fold up in wet weather. The seemingly dead plants survive through the winter. There is also a stemless variety with white flower heads and silvery bracts growing in mountainous regions.

Cleavers Avenue   Cleavers belong to the bedstraw family. The common cleavers is the green, straggling, sticky plant which clings to clothing and animal fur. It has tiny, down-turned prickles on the stem which enable it to do this. From May to September it has clusters of small white flowers. There is also the corn cleavers found in corn fields and the false cleavers, but both are rare in Britain.

Coltsfoot Place   Coltsfoot is of the daisy family. The yellow variety, with heart-shaped leaves, grows on bare waste ground. The smaller purple coltsfoot, with kidney-shaped leaves, is seen in damp, grassy places in the mountains.

Conniburrow Boulevard   A boulevard is a broad, tree-lined road or promenade, more usually in France. The adoption of the word 'boulevard' for the main roads through the estates in Central Milton Keynes was intended to suggest a cosmopolitan atmosphere.

Cranesbill Place   The cranesbill is of the geranium family and has 15 varieties adapted to different growing conditions. The blue meadow cranesbill grows in grassy places, preferably on lime soil, whereas the bright, crimson bloody cranesbill likes dry, grassy dunes. Other varieties come in shades of pink. Its name derives from the long, straight, pointed beak at the tip of the fruit.

Fennel Drive   The herb fennel belongs to the carrot family. It is a tall, greyish, strong-smelling plant with yellow flowers and often grows on waste ground or by the sea. It can grow up to 1.5 metres. The seeds and the roots can be used to relieve flatulence and constipation.

Germander Place   The herb germander was used in monasteries to relieve indigestion and feverishness. There are five varieties: the wood sage and the mountain germander, which have yellow flowers, and the wall, water and cut-leaved germanders which have pretty pink flowers growing in leafy whorls up the stems.

Larkspur Avenue   Of the buttercup family, the larkspur is a short, dainty plant with deep purple flowers with long spurs.

Mallow Gate   The mallow family are all pink and pretty, some small and dainty, others petunia-like as the tree mallow, which is a biennial growing to a height of three metres. The roots of the marsh mallow are used to make marshmallow sweets. Mallows were once used as decorative plants in herb gardens and the dried flowers and leaves used to make an infusion for the relief of sore throats. The Ancient Greeks and Romans believed that the mallow was symbolic of the control of the passions. In medieval monastery gardens it was regarded as a sacred herb because its flowers follow the light of the sun as it moves across the heavens. The monks ate it as a vegetable and it was used as a cure for poisoning and drowsiness and in the treatment of boils, carbuncles and other skin complaints, and mallow tea was made to cure gout – all ailments to which the monks were prone.

Marigold Place   The marigold was a favourite herb in monastic days. It was thought to strengthen the heart and was used to soothe burns and reduce inflamation. The petals were used as decoration in salads. In the infirmary the petals were mixed with goose grease to make a balm which was applied to cuts and insect stings. The marsh marigold is really a buttercup, but the wild, bright yellow corn marigold and the orange field marigold are of the daisy family.

Marjoram Place   Marjoram is a herb of the mint family. Its Latin name is *Origanum vulgare*. The small mauve aromatic flowers grow in loose clusters and were once used to treat rheumatism. The plants were strewn on the stone floors of monasteries and churches to create an aroma. The leaves can be dried and used to make a medicinal cold mixture, and heated sprigs of marjoram applied to aching limbs are said to ease rheumatism.

Milfoil Avenue   Milfoils are waterweeds. They are submerged rooted perennials with feathery leaves. The spiked water milfoil has small pink or red flowers showing above the surface, the whorled water milfoil has greenish-yellow flowers, and the parrot's feather milfoil has white flowers and leafy bracts.

Ramsons Avenue   Ramsons is of the lily family and is similar to the Lily of the Valley. It is a carpeting perennial with white, star-like flowers, long, light green leaves and a scent of garlic.

Speedwell Place   Speedwell is a very common wayside and meadow flower. It has small, vivid blue flowers, like bright blue eyes, and palish green leaves. There are about 25 varieties of speedwell, some grow low and creeping, others straight and taller. Colours range from bright blue to pinkish mauve.

Stonecrop Place   There are 13 varieties in the stonecrop family, their colours ranging from white through various shades of pink, as well as yellow. They are mostly hairless perennials with fleshy, short-stalked leaves and star-like flowers. Some grow in walls and rocky places, others in woodlands, but most prefer a dry, bare landscape.

Teasel Avenue   The teasels include the field, devilsbit and small scabious plants which are not prickly and have clustered pink to purplish flower heads. The well-known teasel, however, is a tall, prickly perennial with pale purple flowers on a conical, spiny head. In winter the dead stems and heads remain after the surrounding vegetation has died down. The prickly heads were once used to tease or comb wool before spinning.

Woodruff Avenue   The white woodruff and the blue woodruff are of the bedstraw family. The blue is an annual which produces its bright blue flower heads cradled in a whorl of leaves from April to June. The white is a perennial with whorls of eliptical leaves and loosely clustered white flower heads, also between April and June. It is a woodland flower and is the more common of the two.

Yarrow Place   Yarrow is a common English wayside plant. It has dark green, divided leaves and white, pink-tinged flowers throughout the summer. In medieval times it was used for healing wounds and as a remedy for nose-bleeds.

DOWNHEAD PARK

Downhead Park takes its name from an existing field, 'Down Head Furlong', shown on Ordnance Survey map 229 and a map of Great Linford 1641.

THEME The Cotswolds

Brockhampton   Owned by the National Trust, the Brockhampton estate and Lower Brockhampton village are two miles east of Bromyard, Worcestershire. There is a late 14th-century moated manor house with a rare example of a half-timbered 15th-century gatehouse. There are also the ruins of a 12th-century chapel and woodland walks include a sculpture trail.

Coberley Close   Coberley is a Gloucestershire Cotswold village in the valley of the river Churn, a few miles south of Cheltenham. The church of St Giles dates from the 14th century, built on Norman and Saxon foundations. It is said that Dick Whittington (c.1358-1423) spent much of his childhood here and in the church there is an effigy of his mother. Dick is believed to have been the youngest son of Sir William Whittington of nearby Pauntly, Gloucestershire.

Colesbourne Drive   Colesbourne in Gloucestershire is the estate village to Colesbourne Park, off the A435 Cheltenham to Cirencester road. Colesbourne snowdrops are famed throughout the forestry and gardening worlds. Henry John Elwes, FRS, was born at Colesbourne Park in 1847 and introduced many new plants, including the snowdrop *Galanthus elwesii* in 1874 which still flowers in the park in early spring.

Cornbury Crescent   Cornbury Park at Charlbury, Oxfordshire is a 400-acre deer park adjacent to Wychwood Forest. It has newly replanted beech avenues, ancient English oak trees and several ancient monuments. The park is owned by Lord Rotherwick and is on the English Heritage register. There has been a house in the park since at least 1337 and the present one provides corporate entertainment facilities, and hosts sporting events and country pursuits.

Daylesford Court   Daylesford House, in the heart of the Gloucestershire Cotswolds, is a late 18th-century mansion in a landscaped park. It was the home of Warren Hastings, Governor General of India, until he died there in 1818. The garden buildings and the lake were designed by John Davenport and the orangery was completed in 1790.

Fairford Crescent   Fairford is a market town in the Gloucestershire Cotswolds. The market place has many 17th- and 18th-century buildings, including hotels and inns from the town's past as a posting stage on the old London to Gloucester coaching route. St Mary's church dates from the 15th and 16th centuries, when it was rebuilt by John and Edmund Thame, and has a unique set of stained-glass windows reputedly by Bernard Flower, master glass painter to Henry VII.

Haythorp Close   A variant spelling of Heythrop. Heythrop Park at the village of Enstone near Chipping Norton is an 18th-century manor house set in 440 acres of parkland. Originally built by the 12th Earl and Duke of Shrewsbury, it was severely damaged by a fire in 1831 and rebuilt and restored in 1869. Today it is a luxury hotel.

Kemble Court   Kemble, Gloucestershire, is a small, very pretty, Cotswold stone village to the south-west of Cirencester. It has a school, church and pub and boasts its own mainline rail link to Paddington, London. There is an ex-military airfield which is now the site of the Bristol Aero Collection. The Red Arrows were based here for several years after they were formed in 1965 and the airfield is still used by light aircraft.

Kirtlington   Near Oxford, Kirtlington Park and pleasure grounds surround the country house. The park was laid out by Lancelot (Capability) Brown in the early 1750s and is now on the English Heritage register.

Mickleton   Mickleton is a small Cotswold village near Chipping Campden, Gloucestershire. In recent years it has become known as the 'home of the Pudding Club'. Founded by a group of enthusiasts in 1985 at the *Three Ways House* hotel, the club's aim is to save the great British pudding from extinction. The hotel bedrooms are decorated in pudding themes – the Sticky Toffee and Date room, the Summer Pudding room, the Spotted Dick room, etc. Puddings such as jam roly-poly and syrup sponge feature on the menus and the club also runs a mail order facility.

Oakley Gardens   Oakley Park at Cirencester was created by Lord Bathurst in the 18th century. The poet, Alexander Pope, was a frequent visitor. Today it is known simply as Cirencester Park.

Sandywell Drive   Sandywell Park is a privately owned mansion set in parkland at Dowdeswell near Cheltenham. In the grounds is a disused railway line and tunnel. In the 1870s the house appears to have been licensed to Dr W.H.O. Sankey for use as a home for the mentally ill.

Stanway Close   Stanway village near Cheltenham contains one of the 'jewels of the Cotswolds', Stanway House gatehouse, which is built of honey-coloured stone. Now the home of Lord Neidpath, the house itself is Jacobean, with a tithe barn, obelisk and restored Baroque water-garden with a 70 ft high fountain. J.M. Barrie, author of *Peter Pan*, stayed there and donated the thatched cricket pavilion.

Tadmarton   In the heart of the Oxfordshire Cotswolds, near Banbury, there is an Upper Tadmarton village with a pub, a church and a church hall, and Lower Tadmarton which is a peaceful little hamlet.

Thorneycroft Lane   Named after the Thorneycroft family of Milcombe Hall, near Banbury, Oxfordshire. The church at the nearby village of Bloxham, has a 'Milcombe' chapel, where the Thorneycrofts are buried. Sir John Thorneycroft, Bart, who died in 1725, was the son of John Thorneycroft, Esq. of Grays Inn.

Warmington Gardens   Warmington village, on the slope of Warmington Hill, is about five miles north-west of Banbury. The church on the hill crest is a prominent landmark and the stone houses are grouped around the village green. The old manor house dates from the 16th century. Two miles distant, Farnborough Hall, an 18th-century mansion, has been home to the Holbech family for 300 years and is now owned by the National Trust.

Windrush Close   In the lower Windrush valley, midway between Oxford and Cheltenham, Windrush is a quiet little village of Cotswold stone cottages. The river Windrush flows through an area which includes Bourton-on-the-Water, where it flows alongside the High Street and is crossed by several stone bridges.

DOWNS BARN

The name Downs Barn was taken from a field called 'the Downes', shown on a 1690 map of Willen, and refers to farm buildings located west of the Great Linford to Woolstone road, shown on Ordnance Survey map 102 of Willen parish.

THEME **Horses**

Bayard Avenue   This has several meanings. A bayard is a bay-coloured horse, or a general term for a special or valuable horse, hence the phrase 'keep Bayard in the stable'. It can also mean a type of blind recklessness or bold ignorance, hence the saying 'bold as a blind Bayard', which probably stems from a French knight called Bayard (1476-1524), who was 'without fear and without reproach'. Thirdly, Bayard was the name of the French paladin Rinaldo's horse in tales of medieval romance. He was a horse of incredible speed whose body (according to legend) would elongate to accommodate up to four riders at a time if required.

Byerley Place   The Byerley Turk was one of the three famous forefathers of the Thoroughbred horse, the others being the Darley Arabian and the Godolphin Arabian. The Byerley Turk was captured from the Turks in battle by Colonel Byerley. At first he used the horse as a charger and rode him at the battle of the Boyne in 1690. Thereafter, this magnificent stallion was put to stud and became the founder of what is known as the Herod line.

Cantle Avenue   The cantle is the raised back part of a saddle.

Capel Drive   Capel is an old (Middle English) name for a horse.

Chapman Avenue   A chapman was a trader or itinerant pedlar of horses and other goods.

Clydesdale Place   The Clydesdale is a breed of heavy horse which has long been bred in the Clyde Valley of Scotland. It is famed for its 'feathered' legs and fetlocks and its high-stepping action. In medieval days, the Clydesdale was bred as a charger to carry armoured knights into battle. Later it became the main source of power to farmers, pulling the plough and the reaper until the invention of the tractor and the combine harvester.

Darley Gate   The Darley Arabian was one of three stallions imported from the Eastern Mediterranean during the reign of Charles II to improve British racing bloodstock. The other two stallions were the Byerley Turk and the Godolphin Arabian and together they were the progenitors of the English Thoroughbred. All modern Thoroughbreds are descended from them in the male line. The Darley Arabian was purchased by Thomas Darley, Consul in Aleppo, who in 1704 sent the horse to his father, Richard Darley of Yorkshire.

Downs Barn Boulevard   This is the main thoroughfare through Downs Barn estate. The French term 'boulevard', meaning a thoroughfare (usually tree-lined), was given to all the estates surrounding the city centre to evoke a cosmopolitan atmosphere.

Farrier Place   A farrier is a horse-shoe maker and fitter. Today, the farrier is also highly trained and skilled in the veterinary care of horses' feet.

Gaskin Court   The gaskin is the upper part of a horse's hind leg, between the thigh and the hock.

Loriner Place   A loriner is a maker of bits, spurs and all metal parts of harness for horse riding and driving.

Martingale Place   A martingale is an item of horse harness. There are various forms such as the running martingale and the standing martingale. They consist of leather straps worn at the front of the horse and attached to the bridle, saddle or girth. They can be used as a restraint and to lower the head-carriage of the horse.

Mullen Avenue   A mullen-mouthed snaffle is a type of bit. It has an unjointed, slightly curved metal bar attached to a ring at each end. It is considered by many riders to be a gentle bit, although some contend that it exerts more pressure on a horse's tongue than a jointed snaffle.

Pannier Place   A pannier is one of a pair of baskets, or bags, slung over the back of a pack animal, such as a horse or donkey.

Pastern Place   The pastern is part of a horse's foot, between the fetlock and the hoof.

Pelham Place   A pelham is a type of bit which is worn with a curb chain, giving more control than a snaffle bit.

Percheron Place   The Percheron is a breed of heavy draught horse, originally bred by a group of farmers in the Perche region of France. Coloured grey or black, it stands around 17 hands high and can weigh up to a ton. It was used for agricultural work, as a coach horse and as an army horse. The Percheron first came into Britain in 1916.

Saddlers Place   A saddler is a saddle maker or seller, a dealer or repairer of saddlery. A saddler can also be a soldier in charge of the cavalry saddles, a saddler-corporal or a saddler-sergeant.

Shannon Court   The shannon (or shin bone) is on the lower hind leg of a horse. The equivalent shin bone on the foreleg is called the cannon bone.

Shire Court   The Shire is a breed of heavy horse. One of the largest horses in the world, it stands 18 hands high, weighs over a ton and is as British as the bulldog. A powerful but gentle beast, it was bred in the Shires of Leicester, Derby and Stafford. Until mechanisation, they were used to plough the land and to pull drays in the towns. Today they are mainly bred by enthusiasts who, thankfully, keep the breed alive for showing at agricultural fairs.

EAGLESTONE

Eaglestone was an existing name of a field, west of Pear Tree bridge in Woughton. An eagle-stone was a hollow stone or fossil, originating in Greek and Roman mythology, believed to have medical powers. Because of debris trapped inside, the stones rattled when shaken and were sometimes found in eagles' nests. This led to the 15th-century belief that eagles' eggs would not hatch without them. The myth continued into the 17th century when it was believed that the eagle-stone helped women to conceive and, if tied to the thigh, ensured an easy birth and speedy delivery. However, it was not to be left in place too long, or the womb would be withdrawn as well. That Eaglestone is the site of Milton Keynes General Hospital is pure coincidence.

THEME **Birds of Prey and Field Names**

Abbotsfield   Named by the developers, Bovis Homes, a field belonging to Mr Thomas Abbot who, in the 18th century, was a major tenant farmer in the parish of Milton Keynes.

Ashby. The Ashby family owned land in this part of Woughton parish during the mid-18th century.

Broad Dean   This is the name of an ancient field and track which once crossed the area. A dean is a wooded valley, habitat of birds of prey such as the sparrowhawk or red kite.

Buckingham Gate   This refers to the area's historic links with the county town of Buckingham. Lords of the local manors were Earls and Dukes of Buckingham across the centuries, such as Walter Giffard, an Earl of Buckingham after the Norman Conquest, and George Villiers, a 17th-century Duke of Buckingham.

Chadwick Drive This is a road on Eaglestone health complex, which includes Milton Keynes General Hospital, nursing homes and clinics. Sir Edwin Chadwick (1800-90) was a British social reformer and pioneer of public sanitary reform. While studying law he worked as a journalist, thus gaining an insight into the appalling living conditions of the poor which, he deduced, were the cause of ill-health. Appointed an assistant Poor Law Commissioner, he laid the foundation for the future system of government inspection and became secretary of the Poor Law Board.

At a local level, John Chadwick was a Surveyor on Bletchley Urban District Council from 1899 until he resigned in 1934. He is credited with having made many improvements to Bletchley, including updating the water supply and sewage disposal arrangements, thereby cutting the mortality rate. An architect in private practice, he designed the Bletchley UDC offices, the schools on the other side of the road and buildings in Fenny Stratford.

Condor Close The condor is a large South American vulture. There are two varieties: the Andean Condor, which has black plumage and white feathers round the neck, and the Californian Condor which is now almost extinct.

Down Dean A narrow wooded valley, perhaps set below somewhere else, such as downstream or down the hillside. A habitat for birds of prey.

Everglade An everglade is a swampy marsh or large shallow lake with vegetation such as rushes and sawgrass, as in the Florida Everglades in America. The Everglade Kite is a species of North American falcon.

Ferndale Suggests the habitat of birds of prey such as the dales where ferns grow.

Fleming Drive This is a road on the site of Milton Keynes General Hospital. Sir Alexander Fleming (1881-1955) was the Scottish bacteriologist who discovered penicillin in 1928. A brilliant medical student, he qualified as a surgeon at St Mary's Hospital, Paddington where he also carried out research in the bacteriological laboratory. He was the first to use anti-typhoid vaccines on people, pioneered a treatment for syphilis and discovered the antiseptic properties of tears and mucus. It was by accident that he discovered the antibiotic powers of the mould (penicillin) growing on a culture of staphylococci. Eleven years later a method of production was perfected and penicillin came into general use in 1942. With two biochemists, Florey and Chain, who had helped in the process, Fleming shared the Nobel Prize for Medicine in 1945, having been elected F.R.S. in 1943 and knighted in 1944.

Forest Rise Named after the forest eagle, which is one of four major groups of eagle in the world, the others being fish eagles, booted eagles and snake eagles.

Golden Drive This refers to the Golden Eagle which, with a length of 80cm and a wing-span of over two metres, is the largest raptor in Britain.

Because its prey includes Red Grouse and other game birds, the eagle has been persecuted mercilessly, almost to extinction. A few may still be seen in the Scottish Highlands but, despite legislation to protect them, they are still killed by gamekeepers. In March they will lay two eggs which hatch several days apart and, usually, the first born chick kills the second.

Great Denson   This was the name of a field, shown on Ordnance Survey map 35.

Griffin Close   The Griffin is a mythical winged monster with an eagle-like head and the body of a lion. It was believed to be sacred to the sun and kept guard over hidden treasures. The Griffin appears in many coats of arms as an emblem of valour.

The Griffin, Eaglestone. A sculpture in concrete by Lesley Bonner.

Harlans Close   The red-tailed or Harlan's hawk is a North American bird of prey.

Harrier Court   There are three varieties of harrier, of which the hen harrier is the most common. The female is larger than the male, measuring 44-52 cm long. They breed on moorland in the north and west of Britain and the male may have a territory of over a square kilometre within which he may keep up to seven mates.

Harrier Drive   The same as Harrier Court. As well as the hen and Montagu harriers, there is the rare marsh harrier. Once commonly seen on Britain's fens and marshes, its numbers plummeted as reedbeds were drained to create farmland and their nests were raided by egg collectors. Other birds were shot, stuffed and displayed in glass cases. Now a protected species, the marsh harrier can be found in the East Anglian fens and marshes.

Hawksmoor Close   Hawk is a general term for any bird of the falcon family, excepting the eagles. A moor is wild, open countryside which provides suitable habitat for hawks.

Kite Hill   The red kite was once very common in Britain but suffered the same persecution as most other birds of prey, until it became almost extinct. Specialised breeding programmes are now gradually re-introducing these magnificent birds into the wild and they have occasionally been seen circling above the fields and woodlands of the Chilterns in Buckinghamshire.

Lampitts Cross   'Cross Lampitts' was the name of a field and old track which crossed the area, and is shown on Ordnance Survey map 128. The name means 'lime pits'.

Lanner Walk   A lanner is a type of female falcon (the male is a lanneret) used in falconry, especially to teach beginners, as it is said to have a 'gentle' temperament. It is slightly smaller than a peregrine and preys on small, hedgerow birds or on members of the crow family.

Market Hill   The houses here were built by Bovis Homes, who named the street. The reason for their choice is unknown, but perhaps it replicates Market Hill in Buckingham.

Merlin Walk   The merlin is Europe's smallest falcon, measuring about 27 cm in length. It lives in open countryside, nests on the ground and preys on small birds. It is often used in falconry.

Montagu Drive   Montagu's harrier was named after Colonel George Montagu, who identified this bird of prey in 1802. Measuring 43-7 cm, it is Britain's rarest harrier, its numbers having steeply declined between 1950 and 1970.

North Ridge   On the north side of Eaglestone on a ridge, the name suggests the habitat of birds of prey such as buzzards or kestrels, which build their nests on crags or ridges.

Osprey Close   The osprey is a magnificent bird which feeds on fish. It spots its prey from the air, dives steeply down to the water and grasps the fish in its talons. The osprey was extinct in Britain in 1916 but since 1954, when a pair returned to the lochs of Scotland, great efforts have been made to encourage and protect them.

Peregrine Close   The peregrine is a large and powerful falcon. In medieval England it was a symbol of royalty and nobility, with harsh penalties inflicted on anyone who harmed it. In more recent times, the peregrine was persecuted and poisoned by chemicals or shot as vermin and its numbers dwindled. In summer they can be seen on craggy coastal cliffs and moorlands. They build their nests on rocky ledges and prey on birds in flight, such as gulls or pigeons.

Whitegate Court. This takes the name of a field, 'Whitegate piece', shown on Ordnance Survey map 129.

FISHERMEAD

*Fishermead takes the name of a field, 'Fisher's Mead', which is shown
on Ordnance Survey map 41, west of the Grand Union canal at Great
Woolstone.*

THEME **Fishing Ports and Villages in Cornwall**

Bossiney Place   Bossiney is a small hamlet of historical interest between
Tintagel and Boscastle. It was once the Parliamentary seat of Sir Francis
Drake. Beautiful, secluded Bossiney Cove has a stretch of sand at low tide
and the coastline includes Elephant Rock and Willapark Head. The Old
Borough House at Bossiney was once the home of playwright and author
J.B. Priestley. According to legend, King Arthur's Round Table rises with a
silver glow on Bossiney Mound on midsummer's eve.

Carrick Road   The Carrick Roads is a wide stretch of water over three miles
long and a mile and a quarter wide between St Mawes and Pill Point. It
is said to be the third largest natural harbour in the world and provides a
deep and safe anchorage for the largest of ships at all states of the tide.

Falmouth Place   Falmouth, south Cornwall's largest seaside town, stands at
the mouth of the river Fal, although the oldest part is on the Penryn river.
Falmouth has always been important, first as a fishing then a commercial
port, and of strategic naval importance. Sir Walter Raleigh first pointed out
its possibilities as a large-scale, deep-water harbour. During the Second
World War, vessels of all sorts were inspected, requisitioned and refitted
here for the purposes of war, such as the shipment of supplies, troops and
equipment. The United States Navy was here in force, as well as British
warships, patrol vessels, hospital ships and minesweepers. Now, in peace-
time, Falmouth is a holiday resort, the port used by fishing craft, ferry boats
and yachts.

Gurnards Avenue   Gurnards Head is on the coast road between Zennor
and Pendeen. There is a hamlet with a hotel on a sharp bend. A pretty
walk between the houses and down a footpath leads to the Head, from
where there are great views northwards to Zennor Head and southwards
to Pendeen Watch. The cliffs here are very beautiful and the challenge
and danger of the rocks attract many rock-climbers. There are relics of the
area's tin-mining past and Gurnards Head copper mine was operating into
the 1830s, using a 20-inch waterwheel. The headland was once an Iron-Age
fortress and excavations have unearthed the remains of hut circles.

Helford Place   Helford river, Helford village, Helford Creek and Helford
Passage are all in the romantic area of Cornwall featured in Daphne du
Maurier's *Frenchman's Creek*. The famous *Ferry Boat Inn* is at Helford
Passage with a group of old cottages. The passenger ferry boat dates from

the 15th century and still runs in summer to the other side of the river, which flows through thickly wooded hills. The area abounds with smuggling legends.

Helston Place   Helston, the main town of the Lizard peninsula, has been an important market town since the days of King Alfred. It was then a walled city with a castle. In Stuart times, the people of Helston petitioned the King in an effort to prevent the building of Falmouth because they feared it would ruin their trade. Helston is famous for its Flora or Furry Dance and Furry Day celebrated in the streets on 8 May each year.

Kellan Drive   Kellan Head is a headland off the north Cornish coast on the coastal path. It can be reached by the path east of the tiny 'deserted' fishing village of Port Quin.

Kernow Crescent   Kernow is the Cornish name for Cornwall. Many Cornish people are campaigning for the restoration of the Cornish language and some of the main roads into the county now display the name Kernow as well as Cornwall on the signposts.

Meadfurlong Middle School. The name is taken from the 'mead' part of Fishermead, which was named after a field called Fisher's Mead. Mead is an old or poetic word for a meadow and a furlong is a unit of length equal to 220 yards.

Mullion Place   Mullion is a sizeable village on the Lizard peninsula and lies a mile inland from Mullion Cove. The cove has a tiny harbour and very rugged scenery, with lichen-covered cliffs and rocks piled upon rocks, with vaults, tunnels, chasms and arches. On fine days Mullion Island can be seen out to sea. It is a mound of land, about a mile round, shaped like a lion couchant. Mullion is perhaps the most typical of Cornish villages, a haven from the violent seas for sailors and fishermen.

Newlyn Place   Newlyn is a fishing village and port on Mount's Bay, near Penzance. It boasts the second largest fishing fleet in the country, which is worth millions of pounds to the Cornish economy. Boats of all sizes, from deep-sea fishing vessels to crab boats and rowing boats, can be seen in Newlyn harbour. The fish market and auction begins at dawn, attracting buyers from abroad. The old Pilchard Works is now a museum. The village, with its granite cottages and narrow alleys, is home to many fishermen and the whole picturesque scene is beloved by artists.

Padstow Avenue   Padstow is a small town on the Camel estuary in north Cornwall. It has narrow streets and a pretty harbour and is best known for its traditional 'Obby 'Oss (hobby-horse) May Day festival. Padstow is decorated with new greenery, bluebells and hazel twigs and the 'Oss, preceded by men dressed in white known as 'teazers', singers, dancers and musicians parade through the town. Believed to be of pagan origin, it is one of the oldest remaining English customs, akin to Helston's Furry Dance.

Padstow has been a boat-building and training port for hundreds of years. A national lobster hatchery is at North Quay.

Pencarrow Place   Between Bodmin and Wadebridge, Pencarrow is a Georgian country house, still owned and lived in by the Molesworth-St Aubyn family who built it some 300 years ago. It stands in 50 acres of woodland gardens which contain 700 varieties of rhododendron. Some 25 miles away and east of Fowey, Pencarrow Head is a headland on the south Cornish coast.

Pengelly Court   Pengelly is a village midway between the north Cornish coast at Tintagel and Camelford at the foot of Bodmin Moor. This area is steeped in the legends of King Arthur.

Penryn Avenue   The Penryn river is one of six rivers that flow into the Falmouth estuary. Penryn, upstream from Falmouth, is famous for its granite works from where stone has been exported to many parts of the world for use in the construction of several famous buildings. Before modern Falmouth was developed, Penryn was the major port of the area. Today it is a busy town with museums, castles, galleries, leisure facilities, yacht clubs, marinas and ferry-boats to Flushing and St Mawes.

Pentewan Gate   Pentewan is a small village five miles south-west of St Austell on the south Cornish coast. It is famed for its Lost Gardens of Heligan, an award-winning 80 acres of pleasure gardens which were restored to their former glory as a living museum of 19th-century horticulture. They include an Italian garden, an alpine ravine, a crystal grotto and 20 acres of sub-tropical 'jungle garden'.

Penwith First School   St Just-in-Penwith is at Lands End on Cape Cornwall. The village boasts the most westerly rugby club in the United Kingdom. Penwith was an important tin-mining area and has relics of mine-workings, left after the price of tin collapsed in 1985. The last mine switched off its pumps in 1991.

Perran Avenue   Perran Sands stretch for nearly three miles across Perran Bay from Perranporth to Ligger Point on the north Cornish coast. A stretch of the sand dunes behind the beach is Ministry of Defence land and is out of bounds but the coastal path diverts around it. The ruins of the tiny sixth-century St Piran's church lie buried in the dunes and a former Second World War top secret listening post is now a youth hostel.

Polmartin Court   Polmartin is the name of a farm deep in the Cornish countryside at Herodsfoot near Liskeard. Polmartin Farm is 'devoted to horses' and its 60 acres are home to some beautiful Pure Arab animals as well as some Thoroughbreds, Welsh Section D ponies and crossbreeds. The owners of the farm specialise in breeding and training the horses for show and for sale.

Polruan Place   Polruan is a picturesque, very old fishing village with the remains of an ancient cross and water well. In south Cornwall, it stands on the estuary of the river Fowey, opposite the town of Fowey. A monument, Punche's Cross, is said to be associated with Pontius Pilate and Joseph of Arimathea who, according to local legend, passed this way with the young Jesus to inspect his tin mines. Polruan ferry crosses to Fowey and is the quickest way over the estuary. Most of the Cornish fishing boats were built here and there is still a working boatyard. Ferryside house was bought by the du Mauriers in 1927; Daphne wrote her first novel here and it is now the home of her son and his family.

Porthleven Place   Porthleven is the first place on the north-west coast of The Lizard. It is a busy little fishing port at the head of a combe and in summer is a tranquil holiday village. In winter, the stretch of the coast between the Lizard and Lands End becomes a shipping trap. Storms in 1912 shifted the silt from the strand between Porthleven and Looe Bar and so much Spanish coinage was discovered from past shipwrecks that the beach earned the name of 'the gold mine'. Porthleven harbour unusually faces south-west into the worst of the winds, so the harbour wall is exceptionally high. The spectacular winter storms bring people to the village to watch the waves crashing over the defences.

Talland Avenue   Talland Bay with Talland village is on the south Cornish coast, north-east from Polperro. Talland Bay is very beautiful, with magnificent rock formations, and has been the scene of many shipwrecks. The sand is mostly only evident at low tide. Stories of smugglers and shipwrecks abound, many of which were spread in the 18th century by Parson Dodge, who was involved in smuggling and told tales of demons and ghosts to keep folk indoors at night.

The Willows First School   The Cornish word for The Willows is Heligan, as in Heligan House and the Lost Gardens of Heligan. (See Tremayne Court and Pentewan Gate.)

Tintagel Court   Tintagel Head, Tintagel Castle and Tintagel village, steeped in the legend of King Arthur, are spectacular features on the wild and rugged north Cornish coast. The ruin on the edge of the cliff was a medieval royal castle built by Richard, Earl of Cornwall, brother of Henry III. Half a mile along the coastal path the Norman church of St Matriana stands high on the cliff top, with the rocks falling sheer to the crashing sea below. In Tintagel village, the old post office is a 14th-century manor house, owned by the National Trust.

Tolcarne Avenue   Tolcarne Beach is a large expanse of sand in Newquay Bay. The crescent-shaped bay is backed by cliffs and is popular with surfers, swimmers and families. There is a surfing school and facilities for snorkelling and fishing, as well as rock pools and cliff walks.

Towan Avenue   Towan means a sandhill in Cornish. Towan beach is at Newquay and is popular for all kinds of beach sports such as sand-boarding, skim-boarding, power kites and kite-surfing, and sand-sailing. The beach is sheltered by Newquay harbour, but a south-westerly offshore wind can produce fast, hollow waves with a swell-size of up to six feet. Towan beach gets very crowded in summer.

Tremayne Court   William Tremayne built Heligan House (of the Lost Gardens) at Pentewan in 1603. It was the seat of the Tremayne family, who controlled over 1,000 acres of land around Pentewan. Henry Hawkins Tremayne, John Tremayne and John Claud Tremayne were botanists and horticulturalists who developed the Gardens of Heligan over the years, and by 1900 had amassed a huge collection of trees, with varieties from all over the world. The name Heligan means the Willows in Cornish.

Trevone Court   Trevone is near Padstow on the north Cornish coast. It is a typical idyllic Cornish holiday village with a pub, a post office, general store, a beach store, a gift shop, a church, a chapel and holiday accommodation. Trevone Bay has a sandy beach set in a cove with many rock pools.

Trispen Court   Trispen village, four miles north of Truro, is now merged with the village of St Erme. Once upon a time, St Erme had the church, school and village hall, while Trispen had the pub, the post office and the chapel. Agriculture was the main employment, but now the village is mainly a dormitory for Truro. The population in 1801 was 358; in 1991 it was 1,255.

Vellan Avenue   Vellan Head is a promontory on the west side of the Lizard, to the north of Kynance Cove on the coastal path. It contributes to some of the best scenery on Cornwall's craggy coastline, high above the wild sea crashing on the rocks below.

Veryan Place   Veryan is a village a mile and a half inland from the south Cornish coast at Veryan Bay. Lying in a wooded valley, it is noted for its thatched and white-washed 'round houses', two of which stand at each end of the village and one in the centre, each with a cross on top. They were built by the Trist family in the early 19th century and, according to tradition, they were round so that there were no corners in which the devil could hide. They are lived in as private houses.

LEADENHALL

Leadenhall is named after a street in the City of London and the Leadenhall Coffee House which once stood there. Leadenhall Street today is the home of Lloyds of London (see Coffee Hall) and Leadenhall Market, which is over 600 years old. Poultry is still sold there, as it has been since 1327. Leadenhall Coffee House was founded about 1661 and was run by Captain Edmund Chillingden, coffee-man. One of the early coffee houses, it survived the Fire of London of 1666. In 1677 a warrant for the arrest of Edmund Chillingden was served, for publishing and dispersing 'false news' along with 12 other coffee-men. The coffee house seems to have been demolished in 1794.

THEME **Leadenhall is adjacent to Coffee Hall and continues the theme of historic London Coffee Houses**

Coles Avenue   Coles Coffee House was in Birchin Lane, Cornhill from at least the beginning of the 18th century. Here in 1701 a Mr Caffarelli, an Italian minister, gave lessons in geography, history, chronology and the use of the globe, three times a week in three different languages. By 1720 auctions of goods such as musical instruments were being held at Jack Coles Coffee House. It was destroyed by the Cornhill fire of 1748 but reopened in new premises in Ball Court, Cornhill by 1770. Seven years later it was being run by Mr Benson and was frequented by merchants and businessmen. The Eagle insurance office was founded in 1807 after 12 businessmen met here to discuss proposals for fire and life insurance. This evolved into Eagle Star and British Dominions Insurance. Coles was listed in trade directories until 1833.

Combes Crescent   Combes Coffee House operated in Bartholomew Lane during the 17th century. There is little information on its activities except that the proprietor, Mr Combes, took up writing news stories as his main livelihood and in December 1679 was summoned before the Council for writing seditious letters.

Fryday Street   There was a Friday Street Coffee House in Friday Street, Cheapside in 1702 of which nothing is known. There were five other coffee houses in the street: Bright's, Hunt's, Townsend's, Vincent's and the White Horse. Little is known of any of them except that Vincent's in 1671 was run by Andrew Vincent, and the White Horse was formerly a tavern or an inn. From 1800-27 it was in use for masonic meetings.

Fulwoods Drive   This is named after Fulwoods Rents, which was a block of buildings in Holborn. There were several coffee houses there, including John's, Squire's, Tom's and Will's. It was an area of London frequented by the clergy, doctors and others of the professional classes.

Ludgate   Ludgate Coffee House was being run by Thomas Stroud in 1667, while another Ludgate Coffee House at Pilgrim Street, Ludgate Hill was run by J. Bishop in 1832. There were several other coffee houses in the Ludgate area, ranging from the American & Continental, to the Turk's Head, and Twining's.

Malbons Court   No evidence of a Malbons coffee house has been found. There was, however, a Malby's Coffee House in Leadenhall, City of London.

Marine Court   Formerly Hains Coffee House, the Marine Coffee House was established in about 1676 in Castle Court, Birchin Lane. It was involved in the sale of ships for the Hudson Bay Company and the setting up of marine insurance schemes. The London Assurance Company was founded here and Royal Charter granted in May 1720, after a payment of £300,000. Scientific lectures and experiments were also conducted at the Marine, as were auctions of commodities such as tea which were purchased by Twinings. The building and the business was destroyed by the Cornhill fire of 1748.

Moorgate   There appears to have been two Moorgate Coffee Houses, one in Fore Street which was opened in about 1680, later pulled down and reopened on a nearby site in about 1750. The other one was opened at Moorfields in about 1805. In 1813 two of its customers, with accomplices, were charged with forging cheques with intent to defraud the banks. Both were tried, found guilty and executed.

Nixons Close   Nixon's Coffee House at the Fetter Lane end of Fleet Street was opened in the late 17th century by a Mr Nixon. After his death in 1713/14, Widow Nixon continued the business with the help of longtime employee Edmund Peele for another year, after which he took it over and it became Peele's Coffee House. Quacks offered their medicines here, and in 1712 one such was advertising the 'World's Beautifyer' which would 'create beauty where Nature had been defective' and, within a week, would cure the worst of red faces in man or woman. He also had a water that would 'bring hair on a bald head' and another to make the hair curl. All this was being offered to tempt 'any person of distinction' who could receive the product by mail order for the lowest price of two guineas.

Palace Square   This is named after Palace Yard, Westminster, which was to the south of Westminster Hall and at one time was divided into New Palace Yard and Old Palace Yard. There were several coffee houses here, the British, Coulsons and the New Exchequer and the Coffee Club of the Rota

Housing in Palace Square, Leadenhall.

to name but a few. In general, they were frequented by Court followers and politicians, both Whigs and Tories.

Phoenix Drive   That mythical bird, the phoenix, which every few years burns itself to ashes and rises again to a new life, is applied to the early coffee houses which perished in the Fire of London in 1666 and rose again from the ashes in the rebuilding programme. Afterwards, fire insurance schemes began to proliferate and their business was conducted in the coffee houses. The Fire Office was opened in 1680 and was later called The Phoenix. It occupied a floor at the Rainbow Coffee House in Fleet Street and was the precursor of the present day Phoenix Assurance Company.

Rainbow Drive   The Rainbow was a common name and sign used for many establishments all over England in the 17th and 18th centuries and in London there were 19 Rainbow Coffee Houses between 1656 and 1839. The Rainbow at Inner Temple Gate was possibly the second coffee house to be set up in 1652 by Mr James Farre. The Rainbow Coffee House in Cornhill ran a Life Assurance Office from 1702 and in 1742 was advertising the services of a visiting 'corn-cutter' (chiropodist). It was destroyed by the Cornhill fire of 1748, but was rebuilt to thrive for another 77 years. At the Rainbow Coffee House in St Martin's Lane, a pest controller sold preparations for the destruction of 'those nauseous vermin called Buggs' and a doctor treated patients with venereal diseases.

Whites Croft   There were two White's Coffee Houses. One near the Royal Exchange was regularly frequented in about 1671 by the notorious Colonel Blood and his friends. Thomas Blood was an adventurer who tried to steal the Crown Jewels from the Tower of London. He failed but was not punished for the attempted crime. As a favourite at Court, he was given some forfeited Irish estates. The other White's Coffee House was in Bedford Court, Covent Garden and specialised in sales of Italian music manuscripts.

Youngman Place   Information on Young Man's Coffee House in Charing Cross is vague and scanty. It seems to have been frequented by 'officers' and its proprietor between 1704 and 1714 was Hester Man. She was succeeded by Bridget Parker, who remained until 1728. By 1742 this coffee house seems to have disappeared.

Woughton Campus

Situated at Leadenhall, but in Woughton parish, this educational area includes Milton Keynes College & Sixth Form Centre, a Recreation Centre and a Sikh Temple which is under construction.

Cottesloe Centre   Cottesloe was one of the Buckinghamshire hundreds. It ran along the west side of Watling Street, south of Great Brickhill and Stoke Hammond and down towards Hockliffe.

Milton Keynes College and Sixth Form Centre, Leadenhall.

St Paul's Roman Catholic Secondary School   Named after St Paul the Apostle, to whom is dedicated St Paul's Cathedral, the City of London's largest and most famous church.

Secklow Centre   Secklow was a north-east Buckinghamshire hundred. It contained most of the designated area of Milton Keynes as well as Stoke Hammond, Calverton and Newport Pagnell.

Sir Frank Markham School   Named after Sir Frank Markham, who lived all his life in the Milton Keynes area and represented Buckingham in Parliament from 1951 to 1964. A historian and biographer, he wrote a *History of Milton Keynes and District* in two volumes and, with Professor F.E. Hyde, *The History of Stony Stratford.* He died in 1975.

LINFORD WOOD

South-west of the village of Great Linford, this was the site of an ancient woodland, a fragment of which survived and is preserved, although surrounded on three sides by light industrial units housing the offices of mainly electronics companies.

THEME **Association with Open Land in England and Wales**

Breckland   Breckland is an area of Norfolk and Suffolk containing much forest and heathland. The name derives from the Old English *brec*, meaning an area in which land has been broken up for cultivation. Breckland encompasses about 400 square miles.

Capital Drive   Not known.

Enfield Chase   Once a hunting forest recorded in Domesday Book, Enfield Chase was divided up in 1777 when it was assigned to the parish of Enfield. It remained common land until further divided by the enclosures of 1803. Most of the woodland was allocated to a Dr Wilkinson who built on it a mansion, Whitewebbs Park, the grounds of which retain a last remaining fragment of Enfield Chase.

Foxhunter Drive   The 'sport' of foxhunting took place across open land until it was banned in February 2005, since when many hunts have converted to drag hunting.

Rockingham Drive   Rockingham Forest in Northamptonshire was once a vast area of woodland where the kings of England hunted the deer. Now it covers 200 square miles of the country between the rivers Welland and Nene.

Sunrise Parkway   This name was apparently linked to the Sun Alliance Insurance Company, whose offices were being built here in the 1980s. Now it can appropriately refer to the Sunrise Coast, the name given to the eastern seaboard between Southwold and Great Yarmouth, which boasts a thousand hours of sunshine a year. Lowestoft is the most easterly town in Britain and witnesses the most spectacular sunrises.

NEATH HILL

The name Neath Hill already existed as the name of a field shown on a 1678 map of Great Linford and Ordnance Survey maps 152, 153, 154, 156 and 219. Also, Long Neath Hill is shown on a Great Linford map of 1641.

THEMES (1) The Tower of London
(2) The City of London Guilds

The trade and craft guilds were set up in medieval times to further the common interests of their members. In London, they evolved from a religious basis, trade or craftsmen who worshipped together forming themselves into organisations of mutual interest for their common good. As the guilds grew in power and momentum, achieving Royal Charters, Coats of Arms, Halls in the City of London and wearing distinctive liveries, they evolved into the City Livery Companies, many of which still exist today. In 1878 they joined the Corporation of the City of London in setting up the City and Guilds of London Institute for the promotion of technical education.

Armourer Drive   Armourers are makers, repairers or custodians of arms and armour. The Guild of St George of the Armourers was formed in 1322 to preserve the monopoly in armour making and to ensure its quality through an apprenticeship system and hallmarking. The Worshipful Company of Armourers and Brasiers, as it is now known, has occupied the same site in the City of London since 1346 and received its Royal Charter from Henry VI in 1453. In 1708 it united with the brasiers (workers in copper and brass) and today carries on the ancient traditions of metal working. It gives charitable support in the educational fields of metallurgy and material science, seeking to encourage young people to study and work in material science, for the benefit of British industry.

Barbers Mews   In medieval days, and for some centuries after, barbers not only cut hair and shaved beards but also performed surgical and medical tasks, including dentistry. Around 1308, the barbers formed a guild and elected Richard the Barber as its Master. Over the years, the barbers and surgeons began to separate and power struggles for control of the guild ensued. The constant battles finally came to a head when in 1800 the Royal College of Surgeons was formed, but by then the barbers' trade had waned and the guild was joined by men of many other professions. Today, the Worshipful Company of Barbers has a strong connection with the medical and surgical professions but little to do with barbery. Almost half the Livery members are surgeons.

Beauchamp Close   The Beauchamp Tower was probably named after Thomas Beauchamp, 3rd Earl of Warwick, who was a prisoner here in the 14th century, during the reign of Richard II. This tower was used for high-ranking prisoners and has some historic graffiti. Before the Spanish Armada, it was full of priests and Roman Catholic noblemen imprisoned by Elizabeth I for plotting against her Protestant regime. Lady Jane Grey's husband, Lord Guildford Dudley, was a prisoner and was taken from here to his execution on Tower Hill in 1554.

Bowyers Mews   Bowyers were makers of bows. Before about 1371, bowyers and fletchers (arrow makers) worked alongside each other, making bows and arrows for use in defence and war. The long-bow was responsible for English victories at Crecy in 1346 and Agincourt in 1415. They originally formed a guild together, but later separated. The rise of the gun in later years extinguished the long-bow as a war weapon and it is now only used in the sport of archery. The Worshipful Company of Bowyers still encourages and supports the craft of bow making and is involved in charitable works. It also has an affiliation with the Royal Navy Type 23 frigate, HMS *Northumberland.*

Broad Arrow Close   Broad Arrow Tower is one of the towers built by Henry III along the inner curtain wall of the Tower of London. It stands on the east side, next to the Constable Tower, and is named after the broad arrow which was stamped on royal supplies denoting royal ownership. From the 14th century, this tower was associated with the Wardrobe, which was responsible for royal supplies. In later years it was a prison and its walls bear the inscriptions of its 16th- and 17th-century inmates. Among these were the tutors of Princess Elizabeth (later Elizabeth I), who was imprisoned here with her Italian tutor by Mary Tudor during the Protestant Uprising.

Byward Close The Byward Tower on either side of the gate-passage overlooks the moat on the south-west corner of the castle. It was built by Edward I at the end of the 13th century and the name probably comes from 'By-the-Ward', although some say that it derives from earliest times when a byword, or password, was needed to gain entry, as is so today. The gatehouse of the outer ward (second curtain wall) was built by Edward I as a new entrance to the west and there used to be a drawbridge and moat which was drained in 1843. The Byward Tower has guardrooms with hooded fireplaces and vaulted stone roofs.

The clock tower at Neath Hill.

Carpenters Court The carpenters first formed themselves into a guild in 1271 and, with the masons, regulated the building trade in the City of London and gave training in the craft through apprenticeships. The Worshipful Company of Carpenters still maintains its original purpose and now runs the Building Crafts College in London, provides scholarships and sponsors craft competitions.

Coachmaker Court The Coachmakers and Coach Harness Makers' Guild existed for many years before receiving its Charter in 1677. With the advent of the motor car, few coachmakers moved with the times and their craft declined, even more so when hand-made motor coach-work was replaced by steel-pressed car bodies. The Worshipful Company of Coachmakers and Coach Harness Makers has been giving prizes for design and workmanship since 1865. In 1884 a prize was awarded for 'a lady's driving phaeton'; in 1897 for a design for a self-propelled light motor carriage; in 1904 for a design for a motor car to carry four people in the hind part and one or two in the front. Today the Company has links with all three armed services, supports the motor car, aircraft and railway industries and has transferred its interests from quality control to charitable associations.

Constable Close   The Constable Tower of the Tower of London was built by Henry III on the east of the inner curtain wall, next to the Martin Tower. It was named after the Constable of the Tower, who today is appointed by the Crown, the keys and custody being delivered by the Royal Chamberlain in a formal ceremony of installation. The Constable has direct access to the sovereign.

Coopers Mews   A cooper is a barrel-maker. He also makes and repairs tubs, casks and other similar containers.

Cordwainer Court   The word cordwainer comes from the Spanish town of Cordoba, which was an ancient centre for the making of a fine, white goatskin leather called cordovan, or cordwain. The craft of cordwaining originally included the making of all leather goods, but became restricted to footwear as other leather crafts formed their own guilds, such as the curriers, tanners and dyers. First formed as a guild in 1272 and receiving its Royal Charter in 1439, the Worshipful Company of Cordwainers today is dedicated to the support of education and training in the design and production of footwear and associated accessories and the promotion of the footwear industry.

Currier Drive   A currier is a leather-dresser. His work entails processing the tanned hides into supple leather to be used for various purposes. The curriers formed themselves into a guild in the 14th century and their craft was officially regulated by the Mayor and Aldermen of the City of London in 1488. By then they had adopted a distinctive livery, heraldic crest and had a Hall in London. Today the Worshipful Company of Curriers has little practical connection with the trade, but pays pensions to leather workers under three ancient Trusts.

Cutlers Mews   Cutlers are makers and sellers of knives and cutlery in general and once included surgical knives. The cutlers first organised themselves into a guild early in the 13th century, receiving their first Charter in 1416. In the early 17th century the cutlery trade became centred in Sheffield but the making of surgical instruments remained in London and now has its own Livery Company. Today the Worshipful Company of Cutlers still has a Hall in London where it fosters apprentices and awards scholarships to Oxford, Cambridge and the City of London School.

Develin Close   At the Tower of London the Develin Tower was built by Edward I (1272-1307) in the south-east corner of the castle. A causeway once led to and from it across the moat, forming a back entrance to the castle. The Develin Tower is not open to the public.

Dyers Mews   Dyers have been dying cloth for centuries and the City of London Dyers formed themselves into a guild in about 1188. With the vintners in about 1483, the dyers were given a royalty of a game (flock) of swans on the Thames. Today, as then, all swans in Britain belong to the monarch, the dyers and the vintners, and the custom of Swan-Upping still takes place each year on the Thames. A flotilla of small boats (including the dyers' boat and the vintners' boat, each 25ft long and flying their companies' banners) paddles the river, rounding up their own cygnets for marking. The dyers' birds are marked with one nick on the beak, the vintners' birds with two nicks and the Queen's cygnets are left unmarked. In 1960, the Worshipful Company of Dyers adopted the 30th Signals Regiment of the Royal Corps of Signals, which now has the emblem of a white swan as its regimental crest. It was the first regular Army unit to be adopted by a City Livery Company.

Fletchers Mews   Fletchers are makers of arrows. To fletch means to feather, from the French word for arrow, *fleche*, so strictly a fletcher adds the flights to arrows, although the term also covers the making of the whole arrow. In 1371 the fletchers appealed to the Lord Mayor for their craft to be divorced from that of the bowyers 'and no man of one trade meddle with the other'. By 1385 the fletchers were supplying thousands of arrows for the Hundred Years War in France. Archery is now a sport and the Worshipful Company of Fletchers continues today.

Founders Mews   A founder is one who works with metal by casting it in a mould. In 1365, when the Founders' Guild was formed, bell founding would have been a major part of their work, given the many churches and cathedrals being built at that time. Today the Worshipful Company of Founders still supports the craft, having recently given a £50,000 benefice to the Central Council of Church Bell Ringers for the equipment and training of bell ringers.

Gilders Mews and Carvers Mews   There has long been a close link between carvers and gilders, the work of skilled wood carvers being decorated with gold by the gilders. Today there are a number of small companies, such as The Carvers and Gilders of London, employing a skilled workforce using traditional methods and materials in both the restoration of old artefacts and the creation of new carved and gilded objects.

Glazier Drive   A glazier today is one who sets glass in windows, but in medieval times the term included glass makers and those who worked with stained glass. The Guild of Glaziers existed in 1328 when glass in ordinary buildings was a luxury item and many churches and cathedrals were being built and decorated with stained-glass windows. So the Glaziers Guild was a powerful organisation and evolved into the Worshipful Company of Glaziers and Painters of Glass which, today, actively supports and encourages the continuation of the craft, as well as providing technical and financial support for restoration and conservation work. One fifth of the members are practising artists.

Gunmakers Court   Gun makers, or gun smiths, make and repair guns or small arms. The Gunmakers' Livery Company was founded in 1637, but opposition, particularly from the Armourers' and Brasiers' Company, delayed their charter's enrollment until 1656.

Innholder Court   Inns, as opposed to taverns, blossomed in the 13th century to cater for the rising number of pilgrims and traders, offering bed and board to travellers and their horses. Once known as hostelers, they became innholders around 1473 and received their first Charter from Henry VIII in 1514 and were granted a Coat of Arms by Charles I. Today the Worshipful Company of Innholders represents all aspects of the hospitality industry and has one of the finest banqueting halls in the City of London. It gives financial support to many charitable organisations including those involved in care of the sick, elderly and ex-servicemen.

Ironmonger Court   An ironmonger is a dealer in or seller of goods made of iron. The Worshipful Company of Ironmongers used to be called the Ferroners Guild, which was existing in 1300. In that year they took action against the Smiths of the Weald of Kent over the quality of iron being supplied for cartwheels in the City of London. They received a Grant of Arms in 1455 and a Charter from Edward IV in 1463. Today the Ironmongers' Company is tenth of the Great Twelve Livery Companies, is owner of the Ironmongers' Hall in London's Barbican and gives charitable educational grants to schools and metallurgy departments of universities.

Lanthorn Close   The Lanthorn Tower was built by Richard I and King John between 1189 and 1216. King John, though unpopular, had a flare for building and decoration. In the reign of Elizabeth I, two priests escaped from the Lanthorn Tower by sliding down a rope from the outer wall into a boat waiting on the Thames.

Martin Close   The Martin Tower was built in the reign of Henry III between 1216-72. He built the inner curtain wall with towers all along it and the Martin Tower stands on the north-east corner. Many Jesuits were imprisoned in the Martin Tower and went to their deaths from there. The name 'Ambrose Rookewoode' is etched in the upper chamber and recalls the Gunpowder Plot of 1605, belonging to one of the conspirators. The Crown Jewels were kept here in 1671 when Colonel Thomas Blood almost succeeded in stealing them.

Peterman Walk   A Peterman was a fisherman, alluding to Peter the apostle, who was one such. Petermen fished the Thames between London and Gravesend.

St Edward Close   Edward the Confessor, King of England from about 1003 to 1066, was canonised in 1161. He was the founder of a new Westminster Abbey which was consecrated in 1065. He was a cousin of William the Conqueror, who built the earlier part of the Tower of London, namely the

White Tower. The St Edward's Crown is one of the Crown Jewels kept at the Tower.

Salters Mews   A salter is a tradesman who makes, deals in or works with salt. Salting was an important trade in medieval times, when it was the only means of preserving meat over the winter. The Salters' Company received its first royal licence in 1394 from Richard II and included in its membership dry salters, who dealt with flax, hemp, logwood, potash and chemical preparations. With the decline of the ancient salt trade, the interests of the Worshipful Company of Salters today are centred on encouraging and supporting chemistry teaching and young people who wish to pursue careers in the chemical and allied industries.

Serjeants Green   A serjeant (or sergeant), in this context, is a court or municipal officer, or a barrister of the highest rank, who has ceremonial duties. Or it may refer to a Serjeant at Arms, who is an officer of a legislative or fraternal body responsible for maintaining order.

Taylors Mews   The Merchant Taylors' Company is one of the Great Twelve Livery Companies. In its Royal Charter granted in 1503 it is described as the Guild of Merchant Taylors of the Fraternity of St John the Baptist in the City of London. Its first Charter, however, was granted by Edward III in 1327, not long after it was founded by a guild of tailors and linen armourers. An allied craft to the tailors, they made the padded tunics worn under suits of armour. By the 16th century there were more merchants than craftsmen among the Company's ranks and a century later there was little connection with tailoring and the Company became philanthropic in character, its interest lying in educational and charitable work. It owns the Merchant Taylors' School at Sandy Lodge as well as a preparatory school, and is associated with five other schools, two of which are also named Merchant Taylors.

Tower Crescent   Named after the Tower of London.

Tower Drive   The Tower of London, a royal fortress on the north bank of the river Thames, east of the City of London, was begun in the 11th century when Bishop Gundulf built the White Tower in 1078. It was added to in later centuries and was a royal palace and state prison until the 17th century. The general outer appearance belies the complexity of towers and buildings within the walls. Among the Tower's famous prisoners were Sir Walter Raleigh, Anne Boleyn, Guy Fawkes, the two young princes who were murdered and, lastly, Rudolph Hess. The Tower today is a barracks, armoury and museum.

Tower Green   Tower Green, within the Tower of London, is the site of the scaffold where so many were executed. Among them were Anne Boleyn, Catherine Howard and Lady Jane Grey (aged 15 years). From a window of the Queen's House overlooking Tower Green, Lady Jane watched her husband being taken from the Beauchamp Tower to his execution, then saw his headless body being taken to the Chapel of St Peter. A short time later she watched as the scaffold was prepared for her own execution. The Yeoman Gaoler's House is next to the Queen's House. Other prisoners were executed on Tower Hill outside the walls of the castle.

Turners Mews   A turner is a craftsman who works a lathe. In olden times wood was turned on lathes to make useful objects, utensils and drinking vessels. Turners working in the City of London in the 12th century formed themselves into a guild and were granted a Royal Charter by James I in 1604. Today, the Worshipful Company of Turners of London still promotes the work of turners by giving bursaries, running competitions and supporting the Register of Professional Turners. They also support regiments of the armed services where turners are employed, particularly REME, HMS Sultan and RAF St Athan.

Vintners Mews   Vintners are wine-sellers and dealers. In the reign of Edward I (1272-1307) the merchants of Gascony had control of the English wine trade, so London vintners formed a guild and took action to secure a monopoly for themselves over the retailing of wine. They also insisted on controlling the quality and measurement of wine. The trade, of course, has never died out and today the Worshipful Company of Vintners maintains some of the old traditions. Early in July the Company processes through the City of London, led by two men in top hats and white smocks who sweep the streets with ancient besom brooms. This tradition goes back to the days when the streets were fouled by all manner of filth and the vintners did not want to slip on the mess. The Vintners, along with the Dyers, are also involved with the ancient ceremonial custom of Swan-Upping. (See Dyers Mews.)

Wakefield Close   The Wakefield Tower is next to the Bloody Tower. It was built by Henry III and guarded the main river gate in the Bloody Tower. Henry VI spent time here during the Wars of the Roses and a marble tablet on the floor reads 'By tradition Henry VI died here on May 21st 1471'. He was killed that night while kneeling in prayer on this spot. Every 21 May flowers are placed in commemoration. Between 1870 and 1967 the Crown Jewels were held in the Wakefield Tower.

Wheelwrights Mews   A wheelwright makes wheels and wheel carriages. It is one of the oldest crafts and the methods of making wheels for horse-drawn wagons and carriages have remained basically the same for 4,000 years. A list of wheelwrights still practising the craft today is held by the Worshipful Company of Wheelwrights, which actively supports and encourages the development of the craft through training schemes. Two Liverymen of the Company are instructors at the Hereford College of Technology.

Whitebaker Court and Brownbaker Court   Breadmaking has been a recognised craft almost since the beginning of time and brown bread made from rye, barley or buckwheat provided a coarse but nutritious food. There are records of a Bakers' Guild in Henry II's reign and from 1155 onwards, but white bread emerged and became more popular during the Middle Ages and the bakers of white bread fell out with the bakers of brown bread and formed a separate guild. The Brown Bakers probably received their first Charter in the early to mid-14th century, while the White Bakers received theirs from Henry VII in 1486. However, with a growing preference for white bread, the Brown Bakers went into decline and in 1645 they re-united with the White Bakers to become the Worshipful Company of Bakers existing today. Still closely involved with the baking trade, most of its 400 members are master bakers and allied traders. They provide scholarships and prizes for young people in the trade and are closely associated with the National Bakery School, a part of South Bank University in London.

NETHERFIELD

This was an existing name of a field, 'Netherfield Close', shown on the central part of Ordnance Survey 47, a map of Simpson in 1781.

THEME **Agriculture, reflecting the work of the Manor. The land in the open field system was laid out in strips of narrow lands and broadlands, which are mirrored in the design of this estate.**

Barnfield Drive   A field with barns on it for the storage of fodder or grain, or for sheltering livestock.

Beadlemead   The beadle was a minor parish official, an officer of the manor court, who acted as an overseer. His job was to keep an eye on the workers and to maintain order.

Broadlands   Broadland was a broad, or wide, strip of land.

Buckland Drive   Buckland, or 'boc-land', is said to have been land held in accordance with the provisions of a royal charter, as opposed to 'folk-land', which was land held under 'folcriht', or common law.

Farmborough   Farmborough means a tract of land used for cultivation or pasturage, along with a house and other buildings. Originally, farms were usually leased or rented.

Farthing Grove   A farthing was a fourth part of anything. In the Middle Ages it was a land measurement, known as 'fardindent'. Farthingland was land of variable size.

Langland Road   Langland was a long, or tongue-shaped, strip of land.

Housing in Farthing Grove, Netherfield, one of the earliest estates to be built in Milton Keynes.

The Hide   A hide in old English law was a variable unit of area of land, but generally about 120 acres and considered enough for a household. Hidage was a tax once assessed on every hide of land. A Norman ploughman was supposed to be able to plough a hide in one working year.

OLDBROOK

Oldbrook is named after Oldbrook and Holbrook fields which are shown on Ordnance Survey maps 136 and 143. The old brook which once ran through the fields is now dried up and hardly recognisable, although its course can be traced running under hawthorn and alder trees, parallel with Shackleton Place, before veering along the north side of the playing field behind Leyland and Johnstone Places. The Cricketers *pub, resembling a cricket pavilion, overlooks the playing field.*

THEME **Cricket**

Appleyard Place   Robert (Bob) Appleyard, born 1924, had a brief career dogged by ill health which led to his retirement only nine years after his first full season for Yorkshire in 1951. He headed the first-class averages that year, taking 200 at 14.14. A medium-paced off-spin bowler of superb line and length, he played only nine tests, heading the averages on a 1954-5 tour of Australia (11 wickets at 20.36) and New Zealand (9 wickets at 8.8). In all, he took 31 test wickets (17.87) and totalled 708 (15.48) in his first-class career.

Arlott Crescent   John Arlott joined the BBC in 1945, succeeding George Orwell as a Producer in the Literary Department of the BBC's External Services. His first cricket commentaries were on the 1946 home test series against India. He continued to broadcast on cricket for more than 40 years. He was also a cricket correspondent for the *Guardian* newspaper and a prolific author. He died in 1991.

Barnes Place   Sydney Francis (Sid) Barnes had a chequered career in league, county and test cricket between 1894 and 1930. A fast-medium seam bowler, he first played for Warwickshire before becoming a professional in the Lancashire League. He was invited to tour Australia in 1901-2, after which he had two full seasons with Lancashire before returning to league cricket. He continued to represent England in tours and tests and was still playing league cricket in his 60s. In first-class cricket, his record stands as 719 wickets (17.09) and 189 test wickets (16.43).

Barrington Mews   K.F. (Ken) Barrington was a Surrey and England batsman who joined the county in 1953 and, during a first-class career which ended in 1968, scored 31,714 runs (45.63). As a leg-break and googly bowler he took 273 wickets (32.61) and held 511 catches. His test career of 82 matches began in 1955: runs 6,806 (58.67), 20 centuries. He died of a heart attack in Barbados in 1981 while Assistant Manager on an England tour of the West Indies.

Blackham Court   John McCarthy Blackham (1854-1932) played for the Australian State of Victoria between 1874 and 1894. He kept wicket in the first test match between Australia and England at Melbourne in 1877 and played a further 34 representative matches during his career, making 60 dismissals (36 caught, 24 stumped) and scoring 800 runs at 15.69. Career figures: 451 dismissals (272 caught, 179 stumped), run aggregate 6,395 (16.78).

Boycott Avenue   Geoffrey Boycott, born 1940, first played for Yorkshire in 1964, his England debut coming two years later against Australia. He was to become both the ultimate professional and a controversial figure due to several battles with cricketing 'authorities', but he graced the game as one of its finest opening batsmen. For his county, he amassed 48,426 runs (56.83), including 151 centuries. In 108 tests he totalled 8,114 runs (47.72).

Brearley Avenue   J.M. (Mike) Brearley. Successively captain of Cambridge University and Middlesex, Brearley was the most successful post-war captain of England. He led in 31 tests, of which 18 were won and only four lost, winning seven of nine series with one drawn. He joined Middlesex in 1961 and, while captaining them for a dozen seasons before his retirement in 1982, they won the championship four times and the Gillette Cup twice. In 454 first-class games he scored 28,168 runs (average 37.84) and 1,442 runs (22.88) in 39 tests.

Bridgeford Court   Bridgford Road in Nottingham runs to the west of the

Trent Bridge ground, home of Nottinghamshire County Cricket Club and one of England's test match venues. Also, West Bridgford, a southern suburb of Nottingham, has its own cricket club.

Cartwright Place   T.W. (Tom) Cartwright was a medium-paced bowler whose career prospered in the county game, but not at test level. Born in 1935, he joined Warwickshire in 1952, taking more than 1,000 wickets in ten seasons. He then coached cricket at Millfield School, played for Somerset, and coached at Glamorgan. He played only five games for England, against Australia in 1964 and South Africa in 1964-5, taking 15 wickets at 36.26. His career record was 1,536 wickets at 19.11 apiece, 13,710 runs (21.32).

Century Avenue   Named after an individual's cricket score of 100 runs.

Dexter Avenue   Edward Ralph (Ted) Dexter was an attacking right-handed batsman who joined Sussex from Cambridge University in 1956 and captained the county from 1960 to 1965. In a 62-match test career from 1958 to 1968 he scored 4,502 runs (47.89), including nine centuries. He scored 51 centuries in his first-class career, totalling 21,150 runs (40.75), and took 419 wickets (29.92).

Douglas Place   J.W.H.T. (Johnny) Douglas, born 1882, joined Essex in 1901. An all-round sportsman, in the early 1900s he was an international athlete, Olympic middleweight boxing gold medalist and represented England as an amateur footballer. He captained the English test team in 1911-12 in Australia and in South Africa in 1913-14, playing 23 games, scoring 962 runs (29.15) and taking 45 wickets (33.02). In his first-class career he scored 24,531 runs (27.90), took 1,894 wickets (23.32) and 330 catches.

Duckworth Court   George Duckworth (1901-66) was a Lancashire and England wicket-keeper who, in a first-class career between 1923 and 1947, totalled 1,090 dismissals, almost one-third of which were stumpings. He toured Australia with the MCC three times between 1928 and 1937 and South Africa in 1930-31. He played 24 Tests, making 60 dismissals, 45 catches and 15 stumpings.

Edrich Avenue   There have been two England test cricketers named Edrich. The elder, William John (Bill), played his first full season for Middlesex in 1937 as a right-handed batsman and fast bowler. His career was interrupted by the Second World War and he became a Squadron Leader with RAF Bomber Command, winning the Distinguished Flying Cross. Returning to cricket, he played until 1958, totalling 36,965 runs, including 86 centuries (42.39), taking 478 wickets (33.31) and 526 catches. In 39 tests he scored 2,440 runs (40.00) and took 41 wickets (41.29). He died in 1986. His first cousin J.H. (John) Edrich was a left-handed batsman who achieved 103 first-class centuries with Surrey between 1959 and 1978, scoring 39,790 runs (45.47). In 77 tests he compiled 5,138 runs (43.54).

Evans Gate   T.G. (Godfrey) Evans, whose career began in 1939 and lasted until 1969, was one of the finest English wicket-keepers and certainly one of the most flamboyant. His dismissals total 1,060 (811 caught, 249 stumped) were later overtaken by his successor at Kent, Alan Knott. Evans was also a creditable batsman, scoring 14,882 first-class runs (21.22). He played in 91 tests, claiming 219 dismissals (173 caught, 46 stumped) and scored 2,439 runs (20.49).

Grace Avenue   Dr William Gilbert (W.G.) Grace. Nearly a century after his death in 1915, he is still one of the best-known names in the cricketing world, after a career spanning 1865 to 1908. He was a colossus, both in the physical sense and in his exploits on the field with bat and ball. Playing for Gloucestershire and London County, this 'father of English cricket' scored 54,896 runs (39.55), including 126 centuries, took 2,876 wickets with his slow, round-arm action (17.99) and 872 catches. In 22 tests he scored 1,098 runs with two centuries (32.29) and took nine wickets (26.22).

Hearne Place   John Thomas Hearne (1867-1944) was a right-arm medium-paced bowler whose aggregate of wickets in a first-class career with Middlesex between 1888 and 1923 was one of the highest achieved. He took 3,061 at 17.76 each and scored 7,205 runs (11.99 average). In 12 tests for England he took 49 wickets (22.08) and scored 129 runs. Among other cricketers named Hearne, John William (1891-1965) played for Middlesex and England, in a career between 1909 and 1936. He was a leg-break and googly bowler and a high-scoring batsman. He played 24 tests, taking 30 wickets (48.73). His first-class figures were 37,252 runs (40.98), including 96 centuries, and 1,839 wickets (24.44).

Hutton Avenue   Sir Leonard (Len) Hutton led English cricket's revival after the Second World War, his career as a brilliant opening batsman having begun in Yorkshire in 1934. Only the second player to be knighted for services to the game (Jack Hobbs was the first), Hutton's prolific run scoring was topped by his 364 made against the Australians at The Oval in 1938. He was the first professional cricketer to captain England and played in 79 tests, totalling 6,971 runs at 56.67, including 19 centuries. In his first-class career, which ended in 1960, he reached 40,141 runs (55.51), with 129 centuries.

Illingworth Place   Raymond (Ray) Illingworth was an outstanding all-round cricketer between 1951 and 1983. After 18 years at Yorkshire, he left in 1969 to captain Leicestershire. In that year he became captain of England and led them 31 times. He bowled accurate right-arm spin, was a useful batsman and good fielder. He became Yorkshire manager in 1979, and captain in 1982 at the age of 50. His career record shows 2,072 wickets at 20.28, and 24,134 runs (28.06). He took 122 wickets for England (31.20) and scored 1,836 runs at 23.24.

Johnston Place   Brian (Jonners) Johnston joined the BBC Outside Broadcasts department in 1945 and began a career as a cricket commentator with both BBC radio and television the following year. His knowledge and love of the game, combined with a schoolboyish sense of humour, endeared him to countless millions of listeners and viewers for more than 40 years. He died in 1994.

Kirkstall Place   Named after Kirkstall Lane, which is adjacent to Old Trafford, the Lancashire County and England test ground in Manchester, one end of which is known as 'the Kirkstall Lane end'.

Laker Court   J.C. (Jim) Laker was a Surrey and England off-spin bowler whose record of 19 wickets for 90 runs in a single test against Australia at Manchester in 1956 may never be equalled. Between 1946 and 1959 he took 1,395 wickets for Surrey (17.37). He played in 46 tests, taking 193 wickets at 21.23 apiece. He retired in 1960 and became a BBC TV cricket commentator. He died in 1986.

Larwood Place   Harold Larwood was the Nottinghamshire and England fast bowler at the centre of the 'Bodyline' controversy during the 1932-3 tour of Australia, which has been described as one of the most bitter and brutal contests in the history of cricket. The tactics of England captain, Douglas Jardine, involved balls bowled at the batsman's body – a ploy which largely featured Larwood, who was never again to play for his country. In 21 tests he took 75 wickets (28.35) and his first-class total was 1,427 at 17.51 each. After retiring, Larwood went to live in Australia.

Leyland Place   Maurice Leyland, hard-hitting Yorkshire batsman who, at The Oval in 1938, hit 187 of England's record score of 903 for 7 against the Australians. He played in 41 tests, scoring 2,764 runs at 46.06, including nine centuries. In his first-class career between 1920 and 1948, he totalled 33,660 runs (40.50), including 80 centuries, and took 466 wickets (29.28). He died in 1967.

MacLaren Court   Archibald Campbell (Archie) MacLaren was a classic, high-scoring batsman who, at different times during his career from 1887 to 1923, captained Lancashire and England. He played 35 tests, scoring 1,931 runs (33.87), including 47 centuries. In first-class cricket he compiled 22,022 runs (34.03). He died in 1944, aged 73.

Milburn Avenue   Colin (Ollie) Milburn was a hard-hitting opening batsman whose career was cut short when he lost his left eye as a result of a car accident. Born in 1940, he came to prominence scoring a century for Durham against the touring Indians. The next year he joined Northamptonshire and was soon a favourite at the county ground. He made his test debut in 1966 but played only nine tests before his accident. He attempted a comeback in 1973 but was forced to retire the following year. His test figures were 654 runs at 46.71, and he totalled 13,262 first-class runs at 33.07.

Oldbrook Boulevard   The main thoroughfare running through the centre, taking the name of the estate.

Rashleigh Place   Canon W. Rashleigh played for Tonbridge and Oxford University before joining Kent in 1885. He played 165 county innings, scoring 4,300 runs at an average of 24.71. He died in 1938.

Rhodes Place   Wilfred Rhodes (1877-1937) was one half of Yorkshire's legendary partnership with George Hirst (1871-1954). Rhodes scored 39,802 runs, including 58 centuries, between 1898 and 1930. As a left-arm slow bowler, Rhodes' career haul was 4,187 at 16.71; and he took 550 catches. In his test career, 58 matches, he scored 2,325 runs (30.19), taking 127 wickets (29.96) and 60 catches.

Richardson Place   Peter Richardson, born 1931, was one of three brothers to play county cricket. He joined Worcestershire in 1949 and in his second full season, in 1953, totalled 2,294 runs (39.55). A left-handed opening bat, he scored more than 2,000 runs in 12 seasons. His aggregate of 26,055 included 44 centuries (34.60). He moved to Kent in 1957, retiring in 1965. In 34 tests he scored 2,061 (37.47), including five centuries.

Shackleton Place   Derek Shackleton, born 1924. A right-arm seam bowler, 'Shack' joined Hampshire in 1948 and produced figures of 2,857 wickets (18.65) and 9,561 runs (14.69) in a first-class career which ended in 1969. He played seven times for England, taking 18 wickets (42.66) and scoring 113 runs (18.83). He was a first-class umpire from 1979 to 1981.

Statham Place   J.B. (Brian) Statham formed two highly successful fast bowling partnerships for England, first with Frank Tyson, then with Fred Trueman. He arrived in first-class cricket in 1950 and made his test debut that winter in New Zealand. He played 70 Tests, taking 252 wickets (24.82). He captained Lancashire from 1965 to 1967, and finished in 1968 with career figures of 2,260 wickets (16.36) and 5,424 runs (10.80).

Strudwick Drive   Herbert (Bert) Strudwick set a world record for dismissals by a wicket-keeper during his career with Surrey from 1902 to 1927. His total of 1,495 comprised 1,241 catches and 254 stumpings. That figure was not surpassed until five years after his death in 1970 (1,527 for J.T. Murray, Middlesex). He also scored 6,445 runs (10.89). His dismissals in 28 tests totalled 72 (60 catches, 12 stumpings). He served Surrey for 60 years, becoming the Scorer on retirement from playing.

Sutcliffe Avenue   Herbert Sutcliffe (1894-1978) was one of cricket's all-time greats. In his first season with Yorkshire in 1919, he scored 1,839 runs (44.85). He was to score more than 1,000 runs a season 24 times before his retirement in 1945, by which time he had amassed 50,138 runs (51.95), scored 149 centuries and taken 469 catches. In 54 tests he averaged 60.73, including 16 centuries. In later life he was a test selector.

The Boundary   The boundary is the edge of the playing area of a cricket ground, usually marked by white lines or ropes.

The Oval   Headquarters of Surrey County Cricket Club since its foundation in 1844, the ground was created from a market garden with the laying of 10,000 turves from Tooting Common. The first Empire team to play at The Oval were the Australians in 1878 and they featured in the first test match there in September 1880. During the Second World War the ground was used as a searchlight site, and when it was derequisitioned in November 1945, the playing area was re-surfaced with 40,000 turves from Gravesend.

Titchmarsh Court   Valentine Adolphus Titchmarsh, born 1853 at Royston, Hertfordshire, played for Marylebone Cricket Club in the 1880s and, after a brief, undistinguished career, became an umpire. He stood in three tests, the first a three-day game between England and Australia at Trent Bridge, Nottingham in June 1899. Titchmarsh continued umpiring until 1905 and died at St Albans two years later, aged 54.

Trueman Place   F.S. (Fred) Trueman, Yorkshire and England fast bowler, nicknamed 'Fiery Fred'. He joined Yorkshire in 1949 at the age of 18 and went on to play in 67 Test matches, beginning in 1952, during which he amassed 307 wickets at 21.57 apiece and 981 runs (13.81). In his first-class career he took 2,304 wickets (average 18.29), scored 9,231 runs (15.56) and took 438 catches. He played a few limited overs games for Derbyshire after leaving Yorkshire in 1968, then became a BBC Radio commentator for *Test Match Special*. He died in 2006.

Tyson Place   Frank Holmes Tyson was the fastest bowler in England in the 1950s, which earned him the nickname of 'Typhoon Tyson'. His brief career began with Northamptonshire in 1952. His pace and bowling action brought him pain and injuries, yet, in only eight years, he took 766 wickets at 20.92 apiece. At test level he formed a partnership with Brian Statham and in 17 games took 76 wickets (18.56). After his 1960 retirement, he emigrated to Australia.

Ulyett Place   George Ulyett, born 1851, was a Yorkshire round-arm pace bowler who made his debut for England in Australia in 1876-7. He had joined the county in 1873 and in a first-class career spanning 21 years scored 20,484 runs (23.47) and took 619 wickets (21.17). In 25 tests he scored 949 runs (24.33) and took 50 wickets (20.40). He died in 1899.

Underwood Place   D.L. (Derek) Underwood's left-arm spin bowling at slow or medium pace earned him the nickname of 'Deadly Derek'. He first played for Kent in 1963 aged 17, and by the time he was 25 had taken his 1,000th wicket, the third youngest player to do so. He retired in the mid-1980s having taken more than 2,500 wickets, scored over 5,000 runs and taken nearly 300 catches in first-class cricket. In tests, beginning in 1966, he took 297 wickets (25.83), and scored 937 runs (11.56).

Verity Place   Hedley Verity. Legendary left-arm spin bowler who began playing for Yorkshire in 1930, aged 25. In 10 seasons before the Second World War he took 1,956 wickets (14.87) and scored 5,603 runs (18.13). He played in 40 tests: 144 wickets (24.37), 669 runs (20.90). He took 15 Australian wickets at Lord's in one day in 1934. In the war, as a Captain in the Green Howards, he was injured in action in Sicily in 1943. He died in a PoW camp on 1 September, exactly four years to the day after his last game for Yorkshire.

Wardle Place   J.H. (Johnny) Wardle was one of the best left-arm spin bowlers in the game throughout his test and county career, which ended abruptly following publication in a national newspaper of his criticism of both his county, Yorkshire, and his team captain. During 12 years of first-class cricket, he took 1,846 wickets at 18.97 apiece, scoring 7,333 runs (16.08). In 28 tests he took 102 wickets (20.39) and scored 653 runs (19.78). He went on to play in the Lancashire League and, later, for Cambridgeshire.

Wynyard Court   Edward George (Teddy) Wynyard (1861-1936) had a first-class career with Hampshire from 1878 to 1912. A hard-hitting right-hand batsman, he totalled 8,407 runs at 34.73, including 14 centuries, and took 66 wickets (28.03). He played only three tests, scoring 72 runs (average 12) and returned 0-17 with the ball.

PEARTREE BRIDGE

Peartree Bridge is named after an ancient bridge crossing the Grand Union canal to Peartree Farm, Woughton-on-the-Green.

THEME **Woughton Parish History**

Ambridge Grove   James Ambridge was a tenant landholder in 1767. In the 1851 census for Great Woolstone, Joseph Ambridge, aged 27, is recorded as a shoemaker. He was married to Lucy and they had two sons and a daughter. At Simpson lived Thomas Ambridge, also a shoemaker, who was married to Mary Ann. They had four daughters and one son between the ages of three and 12 years, all listed as scholars.

Chadds Lane   John Chadd was a local farmer who had land in the North and Middle Fields of Woughton parish in 1745. Another Chadd family, possibly related, were tenant farmers at Willen. Thomas Chadd, who died in 1687, had two children, Mary and Roger, who managed two farms at Willen until his death in 1757.

*Peartree Bridge over the Grand Union canal.
Right: sculpture of a dinosaur constructed in
1979 by artist Bill Billings at Peartree Bridge.*

Hillyer Court   A Hillyer family were tenant landholders in 1768.

Jeeves Close   This was the name of a field shown on the Bletchley Enclosure
Award 1813.

Peartree Lane   Peartree Lane is an old footpath which ran through the
southern end of the estate and led to Pear Tree Farm, which at the turn of
the 20th century was farmed by J.W. Shirley and family. They were also
'corn, cake and manure merchants'. The lane is now a length of redway.

Troutbeck   Edward Troutbeck purchased two-thirds of the manor of
Woughton in about 1717. The Reverend Thomas Troutbeck was rector
of Woughton parish church and took over the manor in 1746. According
to the diary of the Rev. William Cole of Bletchley, on 13 August 1766
Mr Troutbeck of Woughton had three horses stolen from him and, on
17 October that year, Mr Troutbeck gave the Rev. Cole a dozen bottles of
mead, for which he was promised as many bottles of raisin wine in return.

Waterside   So named because it runs beside the Grand Union canal.

Woodley Headland. Wood Lays was the name of a meadow in the south field
of Woughton parish shown on the Woughton Terrier 1745. (A terrier is the
register or inventory of a landed estate.) The name seems to go back a long
way, for a Will de Wodlie is mentioned in 1241.

REDMOOR

Redmoor was the name of a large field shown on a 1781 map of Simpson, Ordnance Survey 184. Once the railway cut right through it, but this now runs to the west of the present site. This small distribution centre close to the Standing Way (H8) grid-road and the A5 trunk road has a parcels sorting office and a food packaging company.

THEME **The Fens**

Dunsby Road. A Lincolnshire village just off the A15, Dunsby lies to the south-east of the waterway known as Forty Foot Drain.

Merton Drive   Merton is a small village near Watton beside Peddar's Way, an ancient Roman road running across the Norfolk fens to the coast at Holme next the Sea. The large mansion, Merton Hall, has been owned by the de Grey family since 1336. Whether they are related to the de Greys of Bletchley is uncertain, but very likely.

Wimblington Drive   A Cambridgeshire village on the A141, Wimblington lies between White Fen and the waterway known as Sixteen Foot Drain.

ROOKSLEY

Named after a field, 'Rooksley Leas', shown on Ordnance Survey maps 191 and 193 as north-east of Loughton Lodge Farm, marked on a 1769 map of Loughton. The Rookes, or Rokys, family were important in Stony Stratford in the 15th and 16th centuries.

THEME **Railway Engines, owing to the proximity of the Railway Station**

Deltic Avenue   The Deltic locomotive is one of the most powerful diesel locomotives ever to run on British Rail's network. It was first built by English Electric in the early 1960s.

Garratt Drive   On the other side of the railway line in West Rooksley, Garratt Drive leads to a carting centre and restaurant. The Beyer-Garratt is a locomotive with an unusual articulated engine. It was devised by Herman William Garratt, a British locomotive engineer, inspector and inventor who, in 1907, proved the merits of his design to Beyer, Peacock locomotive builders. By 1909 the first Beyer-Garratt engines were in production and, as they developed, were used in Australia, South America, Asia and many other parts of the world.

Patriot Drive. The Patriot was a class of steam engine in use between the 1930s and 1960s.

Precedent Drive The Precedent was a famous class of heavy locomotives, better known as 'Jumbos'. London & North Western Railway Precedent Class 2-4-0 'Jumbo' was developed from John Ramsbottom's 2-4-0 'Newton' class, which dated back to 1866.

SPRINGFIELD

Springfield was the name of a field in the parish of Little Woolstone shown on Ordnance Survey map 41.

THEME The Lost Springs and Rivers of London

It is hard to imagine the far distant days when the area now covered by London was a scene of green hills and valleys with rivers and streams running through them. From Roman times at least, these rivers determined the infrastructure of a city that, over 2,000 years, was to swallow the countryside and bury most of the streams and rivers under layer upon layer of successive development and rebuilding.

Belsize Avenue The Belsize was a stream flowing from Belsize Park into the Tyburn at Regents Park.

Beverley Place Beverley Brook is still alive. It flows towards London from Worcester Park to New Malden in Surrey and runs through Wimbledon Common and Putney Lower Common before reaching the Thames somewhere near Putney Bridge.

Billingwell Place No information can be found on this. However, it seems reasonable to suppose that the Billing river once flowed into the Thames at the Billingsgate Market site near London Bridge. The market took its name from one of two river gates in the wall of Roman London. But there are also Billing street names a long way upriver in Fulham. There is nothing to indicate where Billing Well might have been.

Clerkenwell Place Clerk's Well, from which the district of Clerkenwell gets its name, lies at the bottom of some steep steps behind a small door between numbers 14 and 18 Farringdon Road. It was the well used by the parish clerks in charge of the parish churches. Every year the clerks used to gather at the well to perform mystery plays. The well was closed in 1857 and forgotten until rediscovered during excavations in 1924.

Falcon Avenue Falcon Brook was a stream flowing through the Battersea and Wandsworth areas of London. Such names as Falcon Park, Falcon

Road and Falcon Grove in Battersea are clues to this, and the brook possibly entered the Thames near Battersea Bridge.

Graveney Place The Graveney river still flows in south London, through Norbury, Colliers Wood and Streatham to merge with the river Wandle at Tooting. At Norbury it is crossed by the Hermitage bridge where there was once a tollgate, dismantled in the 1880s. The name of the river comes from the lord of the manor between 1154 and 1189, Hamo de Gravenell.

Holywell Place Holywell was a well in the Shoreditch area of London. Holywell Lane and Holywell Row off Worship Street indicate the spot. In the 12th century the waters from it were said to be 'sweet, wholesome and clear', and at that time there were ten other wells in the vicinity, in fact 'wells in every street of the city'. Holywell Priory stood here until it was destroyed during the Reformation.

Kenwood Gate At the north-east corner of Hampstead Heath stands Kenwood House, a mansion designed by Robert Adam in 1767. Before the development of Hampstead began in the 19th century, there were many springs and streams in the area and there was a natural spring near Kenwood House. It therefore seems reasonable to suppose that the house was named after this spring.

Ravensbourne Place The Ravensbourne river has not yet been lost. It rises somewhere in the Bellingham area of south London and flows through Catford and Lewisham on its way to the Thames below the Isle of Dogs at Greenwich.

St Brides Close St Bride was a sixth-century Irish saint. St Bride's church in Fleet Street is probably pre-Norman in origin although it was badly damaged during the Great Fire of London and was rebuilt by Christopher Wren, only to be badly damaged again during the Second World War bombings. Brideswell was one of the City of London's many wells and would have been in the area around St Bride's, such as Bridewell Place and Bride Lane.

Shepherdswell First School Shepherds' well in south Hampstead was the source of the Tyburn. This began as a stream which flowed down from Hampstead to Swiss Cottage.

Springfield Middle School The school is named after the field upon which Springfield estate was built and which determined the theme of the road names. In the London area there were many springs, and probably still are, bubbling away underground. Witness to this are 38 Springfield Roads in the London area, plus numerous Spring Roads, Closes, Gardens, etc.

Stamford Avenue Stamford Brook is truly 'lost'; no information can be found, but there seem to be obvious clues pointing to where it once flowed. In the W6 area of London today there are Stamford Brook Road, Stamford Brook Avenue and Stamford Brook underground station. Nearby, in

Chelsea, Stamford Bridge was possibly a crossing point over the brook.

The Fleet   The Fleet must be the most famous river in London, having given its name to Fleet Street and the notorious Victorian Fleet Prison, so often featured in the novels of Charles Dickens. It rises in the heights of Hampstead to flow through the Holborn valley, under Ludgate Circus and on to the Thames, emerging through a pipe at Blackfriars Bridge. By the 12th century there were settlements along its banks, with St Bride's church and the Kings Fleet Prison built before 1155. By the end of the 13th century, the Fleet was a foul stream of sewage, butchers' waste and rubbish. It was covered over in the 1760s and left as a sewer, which it still is today.

Turnmill Avenue   Turnmill Brook and Turnmill Creek were alternative names for a section of the Fleet river. It was probably the section where Turnmill Street is today, between Clerkenwell and Farringdon. As the Turnmill waters were still fit to drink in medieval London, it was probably a less densely populated area.

Tyburn Avenue   The Tyburn river, rising in Hampstead, flows into the Thames near an old Roman ford at Westminster. Tyburn Springs were roughly where Bond Street is today. After 1236, when the waters of the Thames, Walbrook and Fleet had become too polluted to drink, lead pipes were used to carry fresh water from Tyburn Springs to Charing (then a hamlet), along Fleet Street and up Ludgate Hill to a public conduit in Cheapside. Thus fresh water was supplied, for a fee, to anyone who wanted it. Illegal 'tapping' of the water supply was severely punished.

Walbrook Avenue   The river Walbrook was a tributary of the Thames and one of London's main rivers. Between Roman times and the Middle Ages, it flowed through a valley which was more-or-less where Walbrook Street is today, and was a main source of water supply in medieval London. By about 1460 it had become so polluted and inadequate that it was covered over and forgotten until, in 1954, archaeologists attempting to find the bed of the Walbrook discovered the Roman Temple of Mithras instead. The Walbrook river originally divided the two hills of the city and many historic artefacts have been found along the valley.

Wealdstone Place   Wealdstone Brook still flows from Harrow to Wembley.

TINKERS BRIDGE

Tinkers Bridge is the name of a bridge over the Grand Union canal at Woughton. There was also a field named 'Tinkers Pasture', shown on Ordnance Survey map no. 40.

The Grand Union canal between Tinkers Bridge and Woughton Park.

THEME **The Grand Union Canal**

Aldenham   Aldenham Reservoir, near Watford, Hertfordshire, was built by the Grand Union Canal Company to regulate water levels in the river Colne and to feed the canal. The reservoir is now popular as a sailing, fishing and wind-surfing amenity.

Bascote   Bascote has two staircase locks on the main line of the Grand Union canal in Warwickshire. A staircase consists of two or more adjacent locks where the upper gates of one lock serve as the lower gates of the next.

Blisworth   Blisworth tunnel, 3,056 yards long, cuts through the Northamptonshire hills from Stoke Bruerne to Blisworth. Excavation of the tunnel proved a great deal more difficult than was expected because of problems with flooding, but it was eventually opened in 1805.

Brent   The river Brent at Brentford feeds the Grand Union canal, which crosses the Brent valley by an aqueduct over the North Circular Road. Brent Reservoir was built in 1835 to supplement water supplies.

Broadwater   The Broadwater is a stretch of private moorings on the Regents canal, which is an arm of the Grand Union canal running from Limehouse Basin to Paddington. (There is also a disused Broadwater canal near Lisburn, Northern Ireland.)

Buckby   Buckby Flight is a series of five locks on the Grand Union canal at Long Buckby, Northamptonshire.

Colne   The river Colne feeds the Grand Union canal and merges with it at Croxley Green in Hertfordshire. Plans to build a branch of the Grand Union canal along the Colne valley never materialised. Three aqueducts were built in the early 1880s to carry the Slough Arm of the canal across the Colne valley.

Congreve William Congreve was a scientist who invented a revolutionary new hydro pneumatic double balance lock which was put to use at Hampstead Road lock during the building of the Regents canal in 1814. But the lock was a failure and in 1818 had to be replaced by a conventional design.

Hatton Hatton, on the Grand Union canal, just beyond Warwick, has a flight of 21 locks which take the canal up to 146 feet.

Holmfield Close 'Holmfield' is the name of a house beside the Grand Union canal.

Marshworth This should be **Marsworth** (an error must have occurred in the sign writing), a village near Tring, Hertfordshire. Known as Marsworth Junction to canal users, it is a popular stopping place for the *White Lion* pub, which was once a boatman's tavern. Here the Grand Union canal is taken to the summit of the Chilterns by a flight of seven narrow staircase locks and there is a junction with the Aylesbury Arm of the canal.

Passmore Passmore's Dock is an important private arm of the Grand Union canal at Southall, London.

WINTERHILL

Winterhill takes the name of Winter Hill Furlong, the name of a field partly shown on Ordnance Survey maps 156 and 157 and Loughton map of 1769 south-east of Old Farm. The area is now a trading estate to the south-west of the central shopping centre.

THEME **British Mountain Ranges**

Cairngorm Gate These Scottish mountains lie north-east of the Grampians. Cairn Gorm is 4,084 feet high. The area is popular for winter sports centred at Aviemore.

Grampian Gate The Grampian mountains of Scotland stretch virtually from coast to coast in a south-west to north-easterly direction. The highest peak is Ben Nevis, 4,406 feet.

Snowdon Drive Snowdon, 3,560 feet, is the highest mountain in Wales. Its main peak can be reached by a rack railway climbing up from Llanberis. Snowdonia was designated a National Park in 1951.

WOOLSTONE

Today's Woolstone combines the old villages of Great and Little Woolstone which are recorded in Domesday Book of 1086 as Wlsiestone, *the Anglo-Saxon meaning of which is 'farmstead of a man called Wulfsige'. Although only about half a mile apart, each small village had a church.*

THEME **The History of Great and Little Woolstone Parishes, including the post-Roman period of British History, prompted by the Sites of a Medieval Moat and Medieval Fishponds by the bank of the River Ouzel**

Allison Court A Daniel Allison is referred to in a Buckinghamshire Sessional Records document for Easter 1716.

Ambrose Court This possibly refers to Ambrosius Aurelianus who was born in about AD 435, grandson of the Roman Emperor Constantine. He was a Romano-British soldier who in about 460 organised the British resistance to the Saxon invasion and himself led many battles. It was a period of much fighting and bloodshed and by the time he died, sometime in the 480s, Ambrosius Aurelianus had become recognised as High King by much of Britain.

Butterfield Close William Butterfield was a prominent English architect who designed Great Woolstone Rectory, which was built in 1851 by James Rose of Newport Pagnell. Butterfield (1814-1900) was architect of Keble College, Oxford, St Augustine's College, Canterbury, the chapel and

Nineteenth-century villagers outside the Barge Inn, *Woolstone.*

quadrangle of Rugby School, All Saints' church, Margaret Street, London and St Alban's, Holborn. He was also involved in restoration work which was controversial at the time.

Chislehampton Hugh de Chislehampton was a 13th-century lord of the manor.

Thatched homes in Woolstone, built by Bovis in 1985. Bovis built eight houses, four of which are thatched and the other four built with old brick.

Cloebury Paddock Cloebury Paddock was built on land which belonged to neighbouring Cloebury House, which is a listed building of the early 19th century.

Cowdray Close The Coudray family were lords of the manor of Little Woolstone at some time during the 15th century. Before that, round about the 12th century, the Cowdrays were lords of the manor of the nearby village of Moulsoe.

Eynsham Court Recalling early Briton and Saxon history, Eynsham in Oxfordshire was one of The Four (British) Towns which controlled the valleys between the river Cherwell and Bedford which was attacked in 571 by the West Saxons, who made their incursion not only using the highways left by the Romans, such as Watling Street, but by sailing up the rivers, such as the Ouzel, which flows through Woolstone on its way to the Ouse and would have been deeper and wider than it is today.

Hanscomb Close Ann Hanscomb was a tenant landholder in the late 18th century and the Hanscombs are mentioned on an enclosure map of 1797. A Mr Hanscomb of Newport Pagnell owned the Manor of Little Woolstone in and around 1806.

Kenwell Court Kenwell is a modernisation of the name Caenwealh, who was a Saxon king of Wessex between about AD 642 and 672. The heartland of the kingdom of Wessex was at first in Hampshire but it spread to cover the country south of the Thames from the Kent/Sussex borders to the Tamar river in Devon, and by the middle of the 10th century the kings of Wessex had become the kings of all England and established the roots of the English monarchy.

Lenborough Court Lenborough near Padbury, Buckinghamshire was another of The Four (British) Towns controlling the valleys between the river Cherwell and Bedford at the time of the West Saxon advance eastwards. In 1445 Lenborough House became the seat of the Ingoldsby family, and in the 17th century Parliamentarian Sir Richard Ingoldsby married Oliver Cromwell's daughter, Elizabeth. Today, Lenborough is an isolated hamlet containing little more than Manor Farm.

Linford Lane   This is a section of the old lane which ran from Woolstone, up through Willen, where another section has been retained, and on to Great Linford. Much of the old lane is now a bridleway.

Marshalls Lane   Elizabeth Marshall, aged 65, and her sister Sarah, 63, were lace makers, listed in the 1851 census for Woughton. They were possibly related to James Marshall, shopkeeper and lace maker of Newport Pagnell. According to the same census, Lucy Marshall, aged 15, was a dairy maid working for farmer Levi at Woughton House. She probably belonged to a Marshall family who were all agricultural labourers.

Mill Lane   Mill Lane led to the mill which had been at Little Woolstone since Saxon times. It was still there in the late 19th century and being used to mill flour from William Smith's wheat harvest in the 1870s.

Mordaunts Court   The Manor of Great Woolstone passed from the Staffords to the Mordaunt family in 1642 following a marriage between the two families. The Mordaunts, earls of Peterborough, were lords of the manor of Willen 1490-1640. They also held Buckinghamshire estates at Clifton Reynes and Moulsoe and at Turvey, Bedfordshire.

The village school, Woolstone, where Dorothy Pattison (known as 'Sister Dora') taught the village children in the 1860s.

Newport Road   This is one of the several sections of the old road from Bletchley to Newport Pagnell which have been retained.

Pattison Lane   Dorothy Pattison was the first schoolmistress at Little Woolstone school in 1861. In her late 20s and apparently having auburn hair and hazel eyes, she had left her home in Hauxwell, Yorkshire to escape her crotchety father and took up her post at the newly built Little Woolstone school at a salary of

Holy Trinity Church, Woolstone, built c.1839.

£26. During the three years she was there, she became a popular figure, teaching more than she was bound to teach, creating a choir and voluntarily visiting and tending the sick in both villages. Then she left to join the Sisterhood of the Good Samaritan at Coatham, near Redcar, where she was known as 'Sister Dora'. She went on to become a surgical nurse and died in 1878 while in charge of a hospital in Walsall.

Rectory Fields   Rectory Fields, close to Little Woolstone's early 14th-century Holy Trinity Church, is built on land where the rectory once stood. The Great Woolstone Rectory, built in 1851 by James Rose of Newport Pagnell from designs by William Butterfield, still stands close to the now disused Holy Trinity Church, Great Woolstone, which was built in 1839 on the site of the previous 13th-century church.

Rendlesham   Rendlesham, a village a few miles inland from the Suffolk coast at Orford Ness, was the capital of Saxon East Anglia and site of the royal hall of the Wuffing dynasty of kings. It is not yet known exactly where the hall stood, but it is believed to have been somewhere close to the medieval church of St Gregory where, according to the Venerable Bede, the East Saxon king Swiohelm was baptised in 660.

Talbot Court   The Talbot family were lords of the manor of nearby Mulsoe at some time around the late 12th or 13th centuries.

Tattam Close   Dr Henry Tattam was rector of the parish church of Holy Trinity, Great Woolstone from 1831 to 1849. He was a Coptic scholar (he studied the language of the Copts, Christian descendants of the ancient Egyptians) and in 1830 he wrote *A Compendious Grammar of the Egyptian Language,* followed in 1846 by *The Ancient Coptic Version of the Book of Job.*

Wilford Close   This possibly refers to the village of Wilford, about eight miles south-east of Nottingham, where, according to *Whites Directory 1853*, there may have been a Roman station as a hoard of Roman coins depicting the later emperors was unearthed there in about 1803.

William Smith Close   William Smith of Little Woolstone was the largest landowner in the Woolstones and an enterprising farmer renowned for his desire to improve agricultural methods. The Smith family had owned Church Farm for 200 years before William was born in 1814 and after his father's death in 1837, when he inherited the farm, William began experiments towards the invention of a steam-driven implement for soil cultivation. In 1855 he patented his 'combined double-breasted trench plough and subsoiler', which was purchased by 10 Buckinghamshire farmers and 30 landowners in other counties. By 1862 he had around 200 customers and continued inventing new machinery for another 15 years. After some of his workforce joined a newly formed trade union in 1877, William Smith became disillusioned, stopped inventing, turned his land to pasture and stored his machinery in a barn where it stayed until it was uncovered in 1958. During his lifetime, William Smith also donated the land on which the village school was built in 1861.

WOUGHTON-ON-THE-GREEN

Woughton-on-the-Green is one of the existing villages and is recorded in Domesday Book. Its Anglo-Saxon name was Wuhha's-tun, meaning the place of a man called Wuhha, and the site of the original medieval village has been preserved. Much of this area has been left to grassland and is presently utilised as paddocks.

THEME **The History of the Parish**

Adams Court   The Adams family were farmers in this area. Thomas Adams held land in the 18th century and is recorded as occupying a cottage and garden here in 1769.

Baskerfield Grove   Thomas and John Baskerfield were Woughton landowners living here in the 18th century. Anne Baskerfield, born in 1783, married Thomas Nicholls. The Nicholls family held two parts of Woughton Manor during the 17th and 18th centuries.

Bellis Grove   William Bellis was a landholder in Woughton during the 18th century.

Bowles Place   Born in 1858, Sir Henry Ferryman Bowles, 1st Baronet of Forty Hall, Enfield, was a principal landowner in Woughton. He was MP for Enfield for 24 years and High Sheriff of Middlesex. His daughter, Wilma Mary Garnault Bowles, married Eustace Parker in 1913, and their second son, Derek Henry Parker-Bowles, opened the first phase of the building of Bowles Place in 1965. Sir Henry's cousin, Mrs W. Shirley, became a life tenant of his property in 1936.

Goodman Gardens   The Goodman family were local farmers and landowners during the 18th and 19th centuries. In 1745 George Goodman held land in North, Middle and South Fields of the parish. According to Sir Frank Markham, in his *History of Milton Keynes and District,* John Goodman in the 1760s was the second largest landowner in this area, after Mr Walden Hanmer, Lord of the Manor of Simpson, with whom he had disputes over land enclosures at that time. There were also members of the Goodman family farming at Willen over many years and a butcher called Goodman in Newport Pagnell.

Lucas Place   Nicholas Lucas held land in North and Middle Fields at Woughton in 1745. Henry Lucas was Rector of Holy Trinity Church, Great Woolstone 1704-20.

Newport Road   This is a section of the old road running from Bletchley to Newport Pagnell.

Odell Close   The 'Widow Odell' held land in the Middle Field, Woughton parish in 1745.

The Manor House, Woughton-on-the-Green.

Pinkard Court   William Pinkard was a local farmer and landowner. William Atkins Pinkard was a sponsor for the Parliamentary Act of 30 April 1793 which covered the building of the Grand Junction canal from the Thames at Brentford to Braunston, Northamptonshire, now the Grand Union canal which flows through Woughton.

Rogers Croft   Thomas Rogers was Rector of All Saints' church in the original village of Milton Keynes from about 1445 until 1501. Another Thomas Rogers held land in Woughton parish and had a brickyard at neighbouring Little Woolstone in the 19th century.

The Close   A small corner of Woughton playing fields, this traditional name was probably that of a field, a close being a small, enclosed area of land.

The Green   This is the old village green, around which the old village developed. It remains as an unusually large expanse of grass with most of the old cottages and the manor house grouped around it.

The Greys   The Greys held the manor of Woughton in the early 16th century. A rich and powerful family, connected to the Dukes of Kent by marriage and owning several Buckinghamshire estates, they had held the manor of neighbouring Simpson since 1254. But Henry Grey, who acquired Woughton in 1524, was son of Richard de Grey, a wastrel who brought his branch of the family into disrepute, and Henry never assumed the earldom because he could not afford the £100 he was obliged to pay to the king for the privilege. Descendants of the Greys were the Longuevilles, who retained a one-third part of the advowson into the 18th century.

Turpyn Court   Henry Turpyn was Rector of Woughton's Church of the Assumption of the Blessed Virgin Mary from 1490 to 1493. (According to village legend, Dick Turpin is reputed to have stayed at the early 17th-century *Olde Swan Inn*.)

Verley Close   The Verley family held the two manors of Woughton in the 13th century.

SELECT BIBLIOGRAPHY

AA Book of British Villages, Drive Publications Ltd, 1980

AA Illustrated Guide to Britain, Drive Publications Ltd, 1971

Bendixson, Terence and Platt, John, *Milton Keynes Image and Reality*, Granta Editions, 1992

Chambers Biographical Dictionary, 1986

Clerkin, Maureen (ed.), *World Encyclopaedia of Horses*, Octopus Books Ltd, 1977

Collins Pocket Guide – Wild Flowers of Britain & Northern Europe, Harper Collins, 1996

Edwards, L.A., *Inland Waterways of Great Britain*, Imray Laurie Norie & Wilson, 1985

Elwin, Geoff and King, Cathleen, *Braunston to Brentford*, Blackthorn Publications 1980

Inwood, Stephen, *A History of London*, Macmillan, 1998

Lillywhite, Bryant, *London Coffee Houses*, Allen & Unwin, 1963

Markham, Sir Frank, *History of Milton Keynes and District*, White Crescent Press, 1973

Thomas, Peter Wynn, *Complete History of Cricket Tours*, Hamlyn Publishing Group, 1989

Wisden Cricketers Almanack (various years)

Illustration acknowledgements:

Local Studies Centre, Central Milton Keynes, page 80; Milton Keynes Development Corporation, pages 28, 30, 81. Other photographs are by the author.